DO YOU KNOW
THE AUTHOR OF LIFE?

Joel Wright

Table of Contents

Preface

If you're an experienced Christian, a non-believer, or half in and half out, this book will be able to cover the basics and then lead you into God's fundamental foundations to know His ways.

But firstly, to the non-believer or half in, half out, here is a biblical perspective on why the world is the way it is and what Jesus did for Christians on the cross. This will give you a better understanding of why we believe the things we do!

For the believers, come on a journey with me to help solidify your faith more and express your love toward God in His truths so as to lift you up and see connections to the Old Testament and New Testament. It's a great way to explain and teach friends, family, or one another about how one's soul is in need of a saviour and how Jesus accomplished His Mission of love.

This book will use Youtube links, and if you are reading a printed book, the title of the video will be above the link for you to search on Youtube. Watching the videos will help you search deeper as you go on this journey with me. I highly recommend taking time to watch these videos as they do go well with the content of this book. Although they're not essential, they give a much wider view to understanding the author of life and the realities of Jesus. I will also put all links at the end of the book. This is a journey I want to take you on to change your paradigm about life and for you to enjoy your study for the truth!

I wanted to write a short book about the salvation of one's soul and why we need to know the author of life to be able to be set free from sin and about how important it is to understand what sin is. That will reveal why we need Jesus! I'll try to answer some of life's questions regarding our fallen nature and dissatisfaction in life, and I will also pinpoint where it went wrong for us and direct you to what the Bible reveals and why Jesus is the only way to being truly content and happy in life as you build a relationship with the author of your faith—Jesus!

Many people today in society have heard the name Jesus. Some are curious, some flat out reject His existence, and others use His name as a swear word. It seems it's the norm to use His name in one way or another. I sometimes think about why people don't use the name Buddha as a swear word or Allah, but nope, it's only Jesus! And there is a good reason why that happens, but that's for a later chapter!

Jesus. Jesus, Jesus. We seem not to be able to get away from that name. It is everywhere! It is in Hollywood, in plays, and in the arts! His name is in music. It's on most corners of the earth, whether in a church or someone talking about Him on the street. His name and traditions are associated with weddings and funerals. Our English names are derived from church history and the meanings relate back to Jesus. Our countries are shaped from biblical foundations, and with our constitution, we swear oaths with the Bible!

The church has set up lots of education systems and welfare organisations and shops like the Salvation Army and countless others. Jesus is why we celebrate Easter and Christmas. We have seven days in a week because of God and the weekends revolve around biblical laws and events. People can have Saturday or Sunday off as a rest for the Sabbath day.

Jesus is the foundation of our human rights. You find out in the Bible that the foundations are laid by Him that black or white, female or male are to be treated the same, we are all created in his image.

For there is no partiality with God. (Romans 2:11)

The list can go on, and it's really a paradigm shift. The more you understand the Bible, the more Jesus makes sense and you know why the world we live in is the way it is!

I was raised in a Christian family; my grandfather was a preacher and my father is a preacher. The name of Jesus was normal in my house. But I did not know Jesus **personally** as I was more interested in the things of this world rather than Jesus. I called myself a Christian, but I really did not know much about Him! I was too busy doing my own thing to want to know Jesus.

So this book makes sense for me to write and help you understand that I was in fact naive about Jesus, as He was such a big influence in my life yet

I did not know Him personally. It is a personal choice: either you want to know Him or not!

The Bible says we all do know there is a God, inspired by the Holy Spirit. The Holy Spirit says in the Bible in Romans 1:20-21:

For since the creation of the world His invisible attributes are clearly seen, being understood by the things that are made, even His eternal power and Godhead, so that they are without excuse, because, although they knew God, nor were thankful, but became futile in their thoughts, and their foolish hearts were darkened."

Just like we know how to breathe so we don't need to think about it Or how we learn to walk or talk. We have been designed and hardwired within our DNA to automatically know how to do certain activities! For example, like a bird being pushed out of the nest instinctively knowing how to fly, we humans know instinctively there is a God. That knowledge is placed within our hearts so we know who the true and living God is, but we can suppress that information and we can rebel because of lack of understanding or past hurts or even our prideful nature can try to rule us.

But my question is, do you want to KNOW Him personally as your saviour as He is the faithful one? Isn't there something comforting about knowing there is a higher being out there who is faithful and will be there for you and give you hope, love, and an expected end?

"For I know the thoughts that I think toward you, says the Lord, thoughts of peace and not of evil, to give you a future and a hope. Then you will call upon Me and go and pray to Me, and I will listen to you. And you will seek Me and find *Me*, when you search for Me with all your heart. I will be found by you." (Jeremiah 29:11-14)

Some people say Christianity is for the weak since they need someone to be their help! I tell you I'm glad I have someone to look after me and love me and who cares for me and has given me a purpose.

I find it awesome that there is a destiny for each and every one of us. We are not just random organisms on a planet created by chance. What is the meaning in life created by chance? That does not make sense with how we are incredibly designed right down to the fine details. Or do we create those ideas of life beginning by chance so we can make our own moral standards? Then we can continue doing what we want and be our own judges of morality and do what best suits us for our lifestyles.

Some truth may be simple but can be hard to digest! It takes a bigger person to admit that we have faults. But soon that may make sense to you! Are you still interested in going on this journey with me?

If so, this book will try to explain some hard questions people have had over the years. I will try and direct you to some very simple biblical truths. Some truths can be simple, but I never said they would be easy. Jesus taught the truth and the truth must be stated in confidence. But it's not my own confidence; I use the Bible as the foundation of these claims about the human condition, the fallen nature of sin, why we need a saviour, and how Jesus fulfilled the requirements needed for eternal life.

As you go, you will encounter random names with numbers next to them. If you're not aware, they are books of the Bible and the numbers are how to locate the verse. I was once confused by this a few years ago too. Don't worry; it will get interesting!

CHAPTER 1
Who is Jesus and why did He come?

J esus is the son of God.

Mark 1:11 says: "And a voice came from heaven, 'You are My beloved Son, in whom I am well pleased.'"

The Father sent His son Jesus to come into this world and to be conformed into the image of a humble servant. A king of kings came down to dwell with man in humility to show humans how to love and show kindness. He came with teachings that the world had never heard before. Jesus was teaching one of the leaders of the Jewish people named Nicodemus and said,

"Most assuredly, I say to you, unless one is born of water and the Spirit, he cannot enter the kingdom of God" (John 3:5).

Now it is worth mentioning Jesus was Jewish, and that is very important for later on when we talk about God's law.

Now Nicodemus was confused by that statement and basically said to Jesus, "How can a man be born again? Can I re-enter into my mother's womb?" Now Jesus was not talking about man's flesh being made new but his spirit!

This is the very reason Jesus came for His ministry: to make people's spirits alive so they can enter into the kingdom of God. Now I am not saying your spirit is dead, as it certainly is in you, but your spirit needs the righteousness of Jesus within you to be able to enter into the kingdom of God. Our own efforts cannot obtain this with our own good works. We cannot meet the standards of God's law—there will be more on that later!

The kingdom of God, what is that? And why was Jesus sent so we can go to that place? As we experience this world in our own cities and kingdoms where we live and breathe and have air—the very things we enjoy that God created—well, it's not too hard to imagine a kingdom that is heavenly. That is where God is, and as we are living here on the earth, God and countless others and His angels are living there.

Jesus's main mission was to live a perfect, obedient, holy, and God-abiding life so we can enter into the kingdom of God for eternity. You may say, "Okay, great, He did that and He got in! But how does that relate to me being saved? I'm far from obedient. I've sinned, and I've heard people tell me the Bible says if I sin I will go to hell! Is there hope for me?"

The short answer and a relief: YES, you can be saved! Jesus lived a perfect life for you. We will go into that a bit more, too. That is what makes Christianity different from every other religion. Every other religion involves people doing something in their own self-righteousness to obtain whatever may be promised.

Let's start with Adam and Eve. Yes, Adam from the garden of Eden! It will come in handy to know why Adam is important and how many can be saved. But for now, we will start at the fall. The truth is there is God and there is a devil, and this is where understanding can come in if you understand these two truths. As we know, there is good in this world and there is evil. I will go over some history quickly to give some context!

"In the beginning God created the heavens and the earth" (Genesis 1:1). God created everything we know to be true, and the world was in a perfect state. God said everything He created was very good! God created "the heavens and the earth, and all the host of them, were finished" (Genesis 2:1).

So, God created all things very good, but something went wrong! The Bible says that Satan fell from his appointed place. We skip forward a few thousand years to the prophet Ezekiel, inspired by the Holy Spirit, speaking about the devil's fall.

(Ezekiel 28: 12-19 ESV)

"You were the signet of perfection, full of wisdom and perfect in beauty. You were in Eden, the garden of God; every precious stone was your covering, sardius, topaz, and diamond, beryl, onyx, and jasper, sapphire,emerald, and carbuncle; and crafted in gold were your settings and your engravings. On the day that you were created they were prepared. You were an anointed guardian cherub. I placed you; you were on the holy mountain of God; in the midst of the stones of fire you walked. You were blameless in your ways from the day you were created, till unrighteousness was found in you. In the abundance of your trade you were filled with violence in your midst, and you sinned; so I cast you as a profane thing from the mountain of God, and I destroyed you, O guardian cherub, from the midst of the stones of fire. Your heart was proud because of your beauty; you corrupted your wisdom for the sake of your splendor. I cast you to the ground; I exposed you before kings, to feast their eyes on you. By the multitude of your iniquities, in the unrighteousness of your trade you profaned your sanctuaries; so I brought fire out from your midst; it consumed you, and I turned you to ashes on the earth in the sight of all who saw you. All who know you among the peoples are appalled at you; you have come to a dreadful end and shall be no more forever."

The devil was perfect. He, in fact, was one of the leading, top ranked angels in God's kingdom. Until iniquity was found in him. What was the iniquity found in the devil?

No thanks to Hollywood for making him out to be some sort of equal with God because that's totally not true at all; he is a created being. It's never been a war of good versus evil; it's been a war of redemption for God's people and God's grace and love toward His chosen people, the Hebrews.

Here is the next Bible verse that explains the sin that entered into the devil's heart. Then we will go back to how this makes sense with why Jesus was sent to earth!

"How you are fallen from heaven,
O Lucifer, son of the morning!
How you are cut down to the ground,
You who weakened the nations!
For you have said in your heart:
'I will ascend into heaven,
I will exalt my throne above the stars of God;
I will also sit on the mount of the congregation
On the farthest sides of the north;
I will ascend above the heights of the clouds,
I will be like the Most High.'

Yet you shall be brought down to Sheol
To the lowest depths of the Pit.

"Those who see you will gaze at you,
And consider you, *saying:*
'*Is* this the man who made the earth tremble,
Who shook kingdoms,
Who made the world as a wilderness
And destroyed its cities,
Who did not open the house of his prisoners?'" (Isaiah 14:12-17).

Now we understand that the devil was created and he had a place of power, but he was thrown out of heaven because of his sin that developed in his heart from his will. Into the earth he fell because he wanted to be like God and to be a god over everyone. Being cunning, he had a plan to take over this world and to be the god of this world. In the next chapter, we will learn why and how he did that, and this will get to the point. This is why Jesus needed to come and fulfill His ministry!

Jesus came to this world to set the captives of the devil free. That is the good news of the gospel: for this life to be free and to be forevermore in heaven.

"The Spirit of the Lord God is upon Me,
Because the Lord has anointed Me
To preach good tidings to the poor;
He has sent Me to heal the brokenhearted,
To proclaim liberty to the captives,
And the opening of the prison to those who are bound" (Isaiah 61:1).

Isaiah is talking about Jesus. He was prophesying around 740 BC, hundreds of years before Jesus actually came and fulfilled His ministry. I have one request for you, please look up the two following verses. You can use an old-fashioned paper Bible, but if you only have the internet or a smartphone, you can still find them. Please go find a free app with the Bible. It will only take five seconds to download it and type or scroll in these two Bible verses. As I said, it is a journey together! And it's a journey to knowing the truth, and the truth, the Bible says, will set you free! What is two minutes of knowledge compared to eternity? That's why you're here, right?

Psalm 22 and Isaiah 53

Hint! They're referring to Jesus the suffering Messiah on the cross.

I'll wait. Take your time; I'm just digital ink!

Okay, I put them here just in case you didn't have the internet!

(Psalm 22 ESV)
"My God, my God, why have you forsaken me? Why are you so far from saving me, from the words of my groaning? O my God, I cry by day, but you do not answer, and by night, but I find no rest. Yet you are holy, enthroned on the praises of Israel. In you our fathers trusted; they trusted, and you delivered them. To you they cried and were rescued; in you they trusted and were not put to shame. But I am a worm and not a man, scorned by mankind and despised by the people. All who see me mock me; they make mouths at me; they wag their heads; "He trusts in the LORD; let him deliver him; let him rescue him, for he delights in him!" Yet you are he who took me from the womb; you made me trust you at my mother's breasts. On you was I cast from my birth, and from my mother's womb you have been my God. Be not far from me, for trouble is near, and there is none to help. Many bulls encompass me; strong bulls of Bashan surround me; they open wide their mouths at me, like a ravening and roaring lion. I am poured out like water, and all my bones are out of joint; my heart is like wax; it is melted within my breast; my strength is dried up like a potsherd, and my tongue sticks to my jaws; you lay me in the dust of death. For dogs encompass me; a company of evildoers encircles me; they have pierced my hands and feet, I can count all my bones they stare and gloat over me; they divide my garments among them, and for my clothing they cast lots. But you, O LORD, do not be far off! O you my help, come quickly to my aid! Deliver my soul from the sword, my precious life from the power of the dog! Save me from the mouth of the lion! You have rescued me from the horns of the wild oxen! I will tell of your name to my brothers; in the midst of the congregation I will praise you: You who fear the LORD, praise him! All you offspring of Jacob, glorify him, and stand in awe of him, all you offspring of Israel! For he has not despised or abhorred the affliction of the afflicted, and he has not hidden his face from him, but has heard, when he cried to him. From you comes my praise in the great congregation; my vows I will perform before those who fear him. The afflicted shall eat and be satisfied; those who seek him shall praise

the LORD! May your hearts live forever! All the ends of the earth shall remember and turn to the LORD, and all the families of the nations shall worship before you. For kingship belongs to the LORD, and he rules over the nations. All the prosperous of the earth eat and worship; before him shall bow all who go down to the dust, even the one who could not keep himself alive. Posterity shall serve him; it shall be told of the Lord to the coming generation; they shall come and proclaim his righteousness to a people yet unborn, that he has done it"

(Isaiah 53 ESV)

"Who has believed what he has heard from us? And to whom has the arm of the LORD been revealed? For he grew up before him like a young plant, and like a root out of dry ground; he had no form or majesty that we should look at him, and no beauty that we should desire him. He was despised and rejected by men; a man of sorrows, and acquainted with grief; and as one from whom men hide their faces he was despised, and we esteemed him not. Surely he has borne our griefs and carried our sorrows; yet we esteemed him stricken, smitten by God, and afflicted. But he was wounded for our transgressions; he was crushed for our iniquities; upon him was the chastisement that brought us peace, and with his stripes we are healed. All we like sheep have gone astray; we have turned--every one--to his own way; and the LORD has laid on him the iniquity of us all. He was oppressed, and he was afflicted, yet he opened not his mouth; like a lamb that is led to the slaughter, and like a sheep that before its shearers is silent, so he opened not his mouth. By oppression and judgment he was taken away; and as for his generation, who considered that he was cut off out of the land of the living, stricken for the transgression of my people? And they made his grave with the wicked and with a rich man in his death, although he had done no violence, and there was no deceit in his mouth. Yet it was the will of the LORD to crush him; he has put him to grief; when his soul makes an offering for guilt, he shall see his offspring; he shall prolong his days; the will of the LORD shall prosper in his hand. Out of the anguish of his soul he shall see and be satisfied; by his knowledge shall the righteous one, my servant, make many to be accounted righteous, and he shall bear their iniquities. Therefore I will divide him a portion with the many, and he shall divide the spoil with the strong, because he poured out his soul to death and was numbered with the transgressors; yet he bore the sin of many, and makes intercession for the transgressors."

Pretty amazing! Those two Scriptures make it very clear they are about Jesus on the cross. If you are familiar with the Gospels and eyewitness accounts of the crucifixion of Jesus, those passages should ring a bell. If not, it will enlighten even more understanding for those who want to search one more Scripture and compare it to Psalm 22:18.

"They divide My garments among them,
And for My clothing they cast lots!" (Matthew 27:35).

Not bad for a Bible verse that was written nearly one thousand years before Jesus was even born! The eyewitness accounts of the crucifixion reveal the ancient text's meaning and give understanding about Jesus on the cross. The Dead Sea Scrolls, if you're interested in more research, show reliable dating for most of the Old Testament. The book of Isaiah is well known to historians as being authentic and does date back to those times. There are many gold nuggets in the Bible that will reveal these things. It is in our interest to search out these matters!

"It is the glory of God to conceal a matter,
But the glory of kings *is* to search out a matter" (Proverbs 25:2).

I pray for anyone reading this that God will open their eyes to the Scriptures and the words of God and release that faith upon them so they may understand.

Fun fact: There are more than two thousand fulfilled prophecies and about five hundred unfulfilled (yet to happen) to date. About three hundred of them, Jesus fulfilled during His ministry. One mathematician once went through just eight prophecies in the Bible, and the odds for just eight fulfilments in the Bible is 1 in 100,000,000,000,000,000.

That's like the state of Texas, which is 171.9 million acres, being filled two feet deep with silver coins over the entire area. Then you going into Texas blindfolded to find one gold coin in the midst of the silver coins, and on your first shot, you find the one gold coin out of those silver coins!   - Chuck Missler statistics used.

I know that's a lot of information. Take time for that to sink in and think about it. That's just the odds of eight prophecies being fulfilled, and I just showed you just two of those chapters of the Bible from 750 to 1,000 years before Christ and hundreds of years before crucifixion was even invented!

Now that we have that foundation, we'll get back to the history of the devil and the world with Adam and Eve in the next chapter!

CHAPTER 2
Why do bad things happen?

Now in order to understand why bad things can happen, we must understand the creation of man and the world in Scripture. It has <u>one key</u> answer.

Adam and Eve were made on the sixth day and God created them complete. There is no evolution misinformation here as it is plain and clear that man was made in one day. Going on statistics from how accurate the Scriptures are, I tend to put my faith in God's Word over a mere human's education and incorrect data assumptions. He is our God, the creator of the known universe, and I'm sure He can write an accurate book.

I see it this way: if you don't have all the fundamental foundations of the world and correct scientific data, how can we possibly ever come to a correct answer? If the person does not have the correct data based on false assumptions, how can he possibly have accurate data of evolution?

Chicken or egg, what came first? Or was the chicken created perfectly by a Supreme Being with the power to create such awesome things and to be able create that chicken to lay that famous egg? That seems more logical. Some truths are very simple, but not everyone wants to agree with a God-centred creation because that makes us liable for our actions!

No matter how many times it comes back to creation, it always winds itself back to the beginning with something coming out of nothing. Big bang? I agree, it did start with a big bang as God spoke in Genesis 1:3, "'Let there be light'; and there was light."

Two youtube links here i believe are well balanced approaches to explain and give understanding within the scientific world and they are very interesting to watch.

Science confirms the bible; Ken ham.
https://www.youtube.com/watch?v=CFYswvGoaPU&t=833s

This video and clips within this book are a great source of wealth of information in itself from many years of experienced men of God, and they will help build the foundation that Jesus laid for many; it will definitely give you a better understanding. I highly recommend you watch these videos as you progress through this book, take your time to digest and enjoy. All videos are on the YouTube platform for those with paperback please type in the title given and find the correct videos if possible and enjoy!

The documentary "Is Genesis History?" will answer each aspect of the biblical foundation set in Genesis and will give a well balanced understanding of creation and modern science for anyone wanting to really take their time and enjoy this book with me and be a student for life!

As Albert Einstein said, "Once you stop learning, you start dying." This documentary gets very interesting! It provides an alternative view and can change the paradigm of "acceptable research." You can find it here:

is Genesis history
https://www.youtube.com/watch?v=UM82qxxskZE

My job is to make you think about the claims people tend to hear about as a fact. Then they use these facts to tell others as if they know what they're talking about. We all do it! This includes science data. If you really want to look at a lot of science questions, you will find out the things they cannot explain are theories not proven with evidence! So a lot of educational foundations that are taught to billions of students are theoretical knowledge, not fact, and they're coming from the wisdom of men and leaving God out of relevance and out of mind!

There is also a supernatural element we live in that is widely misunderstood about God and the Holy Spirit and His creative purposes that science cannot fully explain. **Pneumatology** is a great study for healing and tells you about God's creative miracles and how He is the author of life! He knows the very fine intricate details of our universe and quantum physics behind the miraculous!

To get started, I recommend you check out "Pneumatology" by John G Lake on YouTube.
https://www.youtube.com/watch?v=9-DjvIYNe70&list=PLCyk3zOeKL
G5Q9xaaMwjiWyCiHvHnCr9R

I love hearing some of the stories from John G Lake's writings, converted into audio books by God Sounds! It's a great resource and wealth of information from great men of God in the past!

I would be happy if you would do your own research about the Bible and keep an open, unbiased opinion until you find the truth.

It doesn't need to be complicated. God wants us to be as little children seeking His truth and not hardening our hearts in rebellion toward Him. We can choose to simply believe His Word or we can choose to try and find out with our own wisdom and knowledge, but that does not seem to get mankind very far when it comes to great questions of life. The more you let your guard down and start to open your heart toward God and let Him in, the more you will begin to understand the world and the way things are. It starts with simply accepting His words in the Bible: God said the things He created were good!

And God made the beast of the earth according to its kind, cattle according to its kind, and everything that creeps on the earth according to its kind. And God saw that it was **good**" (Genesis 1:25).

Now back to the key verse on why bad things can happen!

Genesis 1:26-28:

"Then God said, 'Let Us make man in Our image, according to Our likeness; let them have dominion over the fish of the sea, over the birds of the air, and over the cattle, over all the earth and over every creeping thing that creeps on the earth.' So God created man in His own image; in the image of God He created him; male and female He created them. Then God blessed them, and God said to them, 'Be fruitful and multiply; fill the earth and subdue it; have dominion over the fish of the sea, over the birds of the air, and over every living thing that moves on the earth.'"

It is important to understand God created everything in perfect harmony until we rebelled against God and sinned.

Genesis 2:15-17:
"Then the Lord God took the man and put him in the garden of Eden to tend and keep it. And the Lord God commanded the man, saying, 'Of every tree of the garden you may freely eat; but of the tree of the knowledge of good and evil you shall not eat, for in the day that you eat of it you shall surely die.'"

God had created all different types of trees with good fruit, but He commanded Adam and Eve not to eat of the tree of knowledge of good and evil. I am of the understanding that God created fruits that gave Adam and Eve intellect and understanding on different aspects of life in the garden of Eden. But God did not want us to know good or evil.

I have to take a timeout here and just think about it. God did not want us to know that there is evil. He wanted only the best for us so as to enjoy every kind of creation He made for us and to be able to live and walk with Him in the garden of Eden with no death and having no knowledge of sin. God made us so we could live with God and enjoy His company!

But Adam and Eve rebelled against God, and it gave God no choice but to separate Himself from us because of sin that had entered into this world.

When man and woman fell from God's holy perfection, we could no longer be in His presence because He is a holy God and a good and pure God who cannot look upon sin. So God, being good and holy, had to allow that punishment that man brought upon himself so God could uphold His order in the universe that He created in righteousness. So in His love and tender mercies, He did a kind act by sending His Son for us as a redemption for the guilty who believe the gospel and turn from their sins and turn to Him and Jesus was the propitiation for our sins.

Romans 2:4:
"Or do you despise the riches of His goodness, forbearance, and longsuffering, not knowing that the goodness of God leads you to repentance?"

Now how did Adam and Eve fall?

They fell from the divine nature, and the heavens were separated from God's holy presence. The harmony of the world fell because of Adam and Eve disobeying God's commandment and giving up their authority to Lucifer, whom they obeyed.

And why did that affect us and this world?

We have fallen with them because we are of Adam's seed. His fallen nature has been imputed into us and we now have a rebellious nature.

Think of it this way. If you put a drop of dye in a clear glass of water, even though it may be a small drop, it will turn the clear, pure glass of water a darker shade when stirred. It will affect the whole glass and make the glass of water dark.

That is how we have all sinned. Since we are tainted with sin, we begin in our old man of Adam's seed, a sinful nature. Once we come of an age to know the difference between good and bad, every one of us has chosen to sin, and to sin is to commit treason against God.

The Bible says we have all <u>fallen short</u> of the glory of God. (See Romans 3:23.) That was the devil's plan from the start, to be a type of god over us. The devil wanted to take humans down to hell with him by deceiving men and women to sin against God, who is rich in mercy and loves us so much He gave His only Son for us. God only prepared hell for the devil and his angels, not intending it to be a place of eternal punishment for man. He says He made heaven big enough for all mankind and He takes no pleasure in those who fall from His grace and go to eternal damnation.

How did the devil start his plan? He entered into a snake in the garden of Eden and spoke to Eve about eating the fruit of the tree of the knowledge of good and evil and said: "'You will not surely die. For God knows that in the day you eat of it your eyes will be opened, and you will be like God, knowing good and evil.'

So when the woman saw that the tree was good for food, that it was pleasant to the eyes and a tree desirable to make one wise she took of its fruit and ate. She also gave it to her husband with her and he ate. Then the eyes of both of them were opened and they knew that they were naked; and they sewed fig leaves together and made themselves coverings" (Genesis 3:4-7).

It is interesting that Adam and Eve did not know they were naked as they had the covering and glory of God upon them until they sinned. They were like little kids naive of their nakedness until they had the knowledge of right and wrong!

Ok, so how does all this relate to why bad things happen? Let's break it down.

Satan wanted to be like God. Satan was kicked out of his place as an anointed cherub angel and fell to earth. Satan saw that man had been given dominion over the earth, as we see again in Genesis 1:26 (emphasis added):

"Then God said, 'Let Us make man in Our image, according to Our likeness; let them have dominion over the fish of the sea, over the birds of the air, and over the cattle, over all the earth and over every creeping thing that creeps on the earth.'"

We were created in the image of God, and God gave us **His image** including dominion over the world He created for us! His image isn't just looking like God but His attributes and nature of authority in every way. In the world He created for us, we are to rule, to be a "type" of god in this world but ultimately be under God's sovereign authority. It's important to note we are not gods but a type of Him. God is the anti-type because God is "I AM." He cannot be like anyone else but Himself! But more on types and shadows soon!

There is a reason why it's called the fall of man as he fell from his dominion when he rebelled against God. He obeyed Satan instead of the only and most high God who he knew to be the true and living God.

Here are some Scriptures that show this truth, that the devil took authority from Adam over this world and allowed evil to rule.

"Satan, who is the god of this world, has blinded the minds of those who don't believe. They are unable to see the glorious light of the Good News" (2 Corinthians 4:4 NLT).

"Jesus said to him, 'It is written again, "You shall not tempt the Lord your God."'

"Again, the devil took Him up on an exceedingly high mountain, and showed Him all the kingdoms of the world and their glory. And he said to Him, 'All these things I will give You if You will fall down and worship me'" (Matthew 4:7-9).

That passage is talking about how the devil was tempting Jesus when He was on His earthly ministry to take back the kingdoms of this world. But He chose to obey the Father's commands and do it the Father's way according to His plans and purposes.

As we look at Scripture, the devil has legally taken sinful people and the world hostage by default from man when Adam fell. Hence, if this world belongs to the devil, then that is why bad things happen: those who are unsaved are slaves of the master of the unsaved world and of those who are in their sins, and whom they obey is who has dominion over them.

"Do you not know that to whom you present yourselves slaves to obey, you are that one's slaves whom you obey, whether of **sin** leading to death, or of **obedience** leading to righteousness?" (Romans 6:16, emphasis added)

To serve yourself or lusts is to serve sin because we are in a fallen nature and we are at enmity against God, but more on that with the law soon!

Now let me set this straight: if you are not saved (yet!), I am not saying you are a devil worshiper; you may not even believe the devil is real! How can you worship him? Well, you're right, the devil would prefer that he is seen as a myth and not real. He is subtle in the way he works into deceiving us that if he isn't real, then God isn't, right? Do you know there is not one atheist demon? They all believe, and they tremble in fear of God because of their wickedness (see James 2:19).

Remember, I said some truths may be simple, yet hard to digest! This is one truth coming up, and it can be hard to accept because of our fallen, prideful nature. We don't like to agree with some truths that can hit home with us. Hey, I said us! Not you! We are all in it together, learning to know humility that God has shown us!

How can the devil try to be a god over us through sinful lusts of our fallen nature?

I have a question for you, Do you like money? I do too! Do you like nice things in life? Sure, why not! Ok, we all like nice things, and I'm not saying being rich or having a successful job is sin or bad! It is a sin only if that becomes first in your life, and it becomes a type of god, above the one and true real God. And if you obey your lusts before you obey your conscience that God has placed there in you, you have now created a god: your own god!

I know it can be very hard for people to make a living and support their family, and it is a must as we all mature and gain understanding in life. I'm not saying you have created a god if you want to support your family! But if you lust after better things and money so you can fuel your life into more material objects, it can be a lustful trap of unhappiness!

But remember who the god of this world is and how he has set certain requirements in our monetary system. Through the lust and greed of men, unfortunately, a few are wealthy and many are poor, and that can equate to struggles in this world with money, housing, food supplies, care, etc. Those issues ultimately come from greed.

One very rich person could feed millions, but it never really happens because they choose lustful objects instead of love for people. Now I'm not saying it's their job if they're rich to be a charity, but it would be good if everyone put each other's needs first; then the world might be completely different!

But for now let's go back to how people can create a god for themselves and how people can so easily be snared in the devil's trap. Lots of people have false gods. Some people carve images and they pray to them for riches, health, and protection. But they were made from man's hands and these images can not see, nor understand nor hear!

Houses can be some people's gods, though I'm not saying they pray to them! But if you are consumed by lust in wanting bigger and more, you can start to serve the things you want and put all your time into achieving what you want and not what God wants for your life. It's God who gives you the satisfaction in life, not objects that don't even know your name!

Some people work and put so much effort into their houses that they have forgotten why they first wanted the house—so that they could live a happy life! But wanting more and more, they can never be satisfied or happy! But that's when lust can come in, and you then want a bigger house and a better car—it never ends! You may think those things can satisfy you, but ultimately it can be empty at the end of the journey.

For another example, I know of someone who is a Christian and he is worth hundreds of millions of dollars. He could feed the homeless and the needy, and he could fund missionaries and bless the church for better education to be equipped to do God's work. He could help people on the streets with drug problems and fund shelters and rehabilitation centers. He could get great reward and love people: people are really where the true value of life is.

But this person wants to become a billionaire! And he is so close, yet he is poor because he wants to reach that milestone, so he doesn't spend anything unless it can be of gain to him to reach his goal. Now I'm not saying wanting to be a billionaire is a sin. Go for it! But if it holds you back for greed of status as this person seems to be doing, you have now created a god in your life and that god is called pride (aka status)! That's the same sin that caused the devil to fall! He obeys his lust over his conscience to help people, and to love people is what God has asked all of us to do to fulfill the greatest commandment: to love one another as He has loved us!

You are who you worship. If you worship fashion, you will become vain and empty. If you worship money, you will become greedy. It has a trickle-down effect on your personality; with whatever you worship, you will eventually want to become like it because that is where you put all your energy and focus!

So, the devil is cunning and becomes many things to many people in the form of lust, and it's important not to fall into that trap! Now clearly money and items are not the devil, but in the mind, they can become lusts. The Bible says full-grown lust leads to death (see James 1:15). Passions can lead you to sin to get what you want. That can then slowly degrade your morals or compassion for the sake of gain.

The Bible teaches that if you are in your sins and have not accepted Jesus as your saviour, you are then considered to be in agreement with the devil's plan for your life. I can understand why people in this world can be hurt if they are being led astray in error and wrong desires—that's how Adam and Eve fell, through lust and desire! The devil has not changed his tactics.

He knows humans well enough to become subtle to encourage our minds to desire things, and over time, we can be hardened in life from failed experiences, letdowns, or not achieving what we thought we wanted.

I used money in my example, but it can be in any form. Money and houses are often the easiest way to relate to people. For example, if you worship religion, you will become self-righteous and think you are above everyone for status, just like the Pharisees in the Bible. They were so puffed up with pride that they were blinded from being able to repent because they thought they were perfect. They are the ones the devil used to crucify Jesus, those who were His own chosen people according to the flesh from the tribes of Israel according to the natural offspring!

"Now to Abraham and his Seed were the promises made. He does not say, 'And to seeds,' as of many, but as of one, 'And to your Seed,' who is Christ" (Galatians 3:16).

Jesus made spiritual offspring too! I will cover that later; back to whom we worship!

On the bright side, we can become good from what we worship too. The Bible says we should worship Jesus and Him only. I think that is cool as we can become love as we take on His qualities of grace, peace, and understanding. We are to be slow to anger with each other. The devil first got into trouble because he wanted to be like God, but that was not for him to decide. The Father has given us that privilege, we who have the lowest rank in the known universe and are made out of dirt! We are under the angels to be like the very God who is love.

That is the first step on this journey with me to understand why we need a saviour, Jesus Christ, the righteous one. This is what He accomplished on His earthly ministry to take back dominion from the devil and cleanse us of our sins.

CHAPTER 3
What is God's law?

Before getting into this, I want to express to you this is not me judging you nor is this chapter about condemning you. That is for God only to judge as He is the only one who can see all the motives of our hearts. This chapter is aimed to show our true selves like a mirror shows us a reflection!

We are going to look at the commandments and reflect on how good and holy the Ten Commandments are. We will learn how God has standards that He once expected mankind to keep in the old covenant. I'll get back to the mirror analogy at the end of the chapter, but for now, let's jump in!

Have you ever heard of the Ten Commandments? Most people have heard of the Ten Commandments either in movies or through someone using it as an expression.

To understand why we need a saviour, we must go into the law God gave to Moses in Exodus 20 in the Bible.
"I am the Lord your God, who brought you out of the land of Egypt, out of the house of bondage.
"You shall have no other gods before Me.
"You shall not make for yourself a carved image—any likeness of anything that is in heaven above, or that is in the earth beneath, or that is in the water under the earth; you shall not bow down to them nor serve them. For I, the Lord your God, am a jealous God, visiting the iniquity of the fathers upon the children to the third and fourth generations of those who hate Me, but showing mercy to thousands, to those who love Me and keep My commandments.
"You shall not take the name of the Lord your God in vain, for the Lord will not hold him guiltless who takes His name in vain.
"Remember the Sabbath day, to keep it holy. Six days you shall labor and do all your work, but the seventh day is the Sabbath of the Lord your God. In it you shall do no work: you, nor your son, nor your daughter, nor your male servant, nor your female servant, nor your cattle, nor your stranger who is within your gates. For in six days the Lord made the heavens and

the earth, the sea, and all that is in them, and rested the seventh day. Therefore the Lord blessed the Sabbath day and hallowed it.

"Honor your father and your mother, that your days may be long upon the land which the Lord your God is giving you.

"You shall not murder.

"You shall not commit adultery.

"You shall not steal.

"You shall not bear false witness against your neighbor.

"You shall not covet your neighbor's house; you shall not covet your neighbor's wife, nor his male servant, nor his female servant, nor his ox, nor his donkey, nor anything that is your neighbor's" (Exodus 20:2-17).

God gave His Hebrew people these Ten Commandments. He also gave, in total, 613 commandments that they should obey throughout the books of Moses. That's quite a lot, I know!

I'll let you in on a secret. God knew His Hebrew people could not keep these commandments, even though He did expect them to try and keep them! That's the second step in the right direction in understanding why we need a saviour. You may be thinking, "Now you keep mentioning His Hebrew people, but I'm not Jewish. Well, not that I know of!" But that's an interesting study by itself, the diaspora, where the tribes ended up scattered around the world!

Quick summary! And this time I'll keep it short! Well, I'll try ...

- God chose a man in this world to establish a people set aside for Himself.

- God promised Abraham He would give him lots of children: in fact, as many as the stars in the sky that Abraham could see or the sand grains on the shore. Even though Sarah, his wife, couldn't as she was barren!

- God saw Abraham and had mercy on him and chose to love him. God tested Abraham, and Abraham was faithful and obeyed God.

- God then blessed him and made Abraham great in wealth and gave him a very big family. That is where the Hebrews come from.· God made promises to Abraham, and God is faithful to fulfill His promises. This is important to understand who Jesus is and why He was sent for the salvation of the heirs of the promised **seed** from Abraham, but what if you're not Hebrew? Is there still salvation for you? Yes! Jesus made a way for everyone to be made a part of the spiritual seed. Remember how I said Jesus made a spiritual seed? We will touch on that soon!

Phew, okay! I think that sums it up quickly. God had favour on Abraham. Awesome! Now back to the law.

Imagine you are hanging over a cliff that leads to an eternity of punishment and you are linked with a harness on a chain with ten links. Now, if you break one of those links in the chain, will the other unbroken links still save you? No, of course not! If one link breaks, regardless of the order, you're going down!

Okay, I want to ask a question! Have you ever rebelled against one of those Ten Commandments? Yes? Me too ... So where does that leave us? In need of Jesus Christ. That is why Jesus is so important. He came and lived a perfect and sinless life, and He fulfilled the Father's 613 commandments perfectly for us!

Now I want to bring your attention back to Adam in the garden of Eden. The Bible states through ONE's sin (Adam), death entered into the world through one man's disobedience. Well, ONE's obedience (Jesus Christ) brought life into the world and the redemption of believers' souls and bodies.

"Therefore, just as through one man, sin entered the world and death through sin, thus death spread to all men, because all sinned— (For until the law, sin was in the world, but sin is not imputed when there is no law). Nevertheless, death reigned from Adam to Moses, even over those who had not sinned according to the likeness of the transgression of Adam, who is a type of Him who was to come [Jesus]. But the free gift is not like the offense. For if by one man's offense many died, much more the grace of God and the gift by the grace of the one Man, Jesus Christ, abounded to many. And the gift is not like that which came through the one who sinned. For the judgment which came from one offense resulted in condemnation, but the free gift which came from many offenses resulted in justification. For if by the one man's offense death reigned through the one, much more those who receive abundance of grace and of the gift of righteousness will reign in life through the One, Jesus Christ.)

"Therefore, as through one man's offense judgment came to all men, resulting in condemnation, even so through one Man's righteous act the free gift came to all men, resulting in justification of life. For as by one man's disobedience many were made sinners, so also by one Man's obedience many will be made righteous.

"Moreover, the law entered that the offense might abound. But where sin abounded, grace abounded much more, so that as sin reigned in death, even so grace might reign through righteousness to eternal life through Jesus Christ our Lord" (Romans 5:12-21, emphasis added).

"Since by man came death, by Man also came the resurrection of the dead. For as in Adam all die, even so in Christ all shall be made alive" (1 Corinthians 15:21-22).

You may say, "Okay, Joel, so you're telling me that since Adam sinned as one man's act and many in this world now have the knowledge to do good or evil, that disobedience then allowed death to enter into the world?" Yes, that's it, but since God is just and fair, in His grace He made a way for one man's works (aka good deeds) to make many people righteous! Oh, the manifold ways God works!

So, back to the law. The law is there to show us we cannot keep God's commandments. Like a mirror reflects our appearance, the law reflects our behaviour. It teaches us that we are sinful and not perfect, but, in fact, we need help. So it is not our own good deeds that will get us to heaven, but by grace you have been (or can be) saved by faith in Jesus!

CHAPTER 4
What is sin?

I want to express this is not about condemning anyone, but it is important to know what sin is in God's eyes versus our standard of it. Sin is important to identify so we know how to treat it. How would you know how to treat sin unless you are made more aware that Jesus is the only way to address the issue of sin? You also have to know that sin can create life's problems, and the final fix for sin is what Jesus did for us!

We all know what sin is, but there are very different perceptions of sin. We can very much be conditioned to our environments. For example, let's have a quick look at the 1950s. Let's have a look at a few beliefs from back then and then let's judge them from today's moral standards of living and what was socially acceptable back then. If we fast forward seventy years, our standards, or what are socially accepted morals, have been in a steep decline.

American Hollywood! Well, it was at its peak and emerging into the world in the 1950s. American culture was everywhere. Country and westerns, long fancy rocket shaped cars, Johnny Cash, and Elvis! It was an overflow into the world of influence. Everyone around the world wanted to have that lifestyle: prosperous, peaceful, rich, and fun! It shaped cultures around the world.

We still see it today: Asian, white, black, all people in between, the Kardashians! Look at how a lot of culture revolves around these celebrities. What we put into our minds is what will shape us. Have you ever made a new friend, and months later after hanging out, you start to make gestures or use a saying he or she says, but before you met them you never did that?

It is how we are wired; we are shaped by our surroundings!

The 1950s really came from a generation that experienced hard times. When they were children, there were wars. World War I for some and World War II for others. Many went through the Great Depression in 1929. This generation who hit the 1950s were middle aged. They had witnessed a lot of horrific times, but they were also very much at the end of some revival waves from people like Smith Wigglesworth, Kathryn Kuhlman, and John G Lake! If you would like to look into these great men and women of God, I would really, really impress upon you to do so. Roberts Liardon has made short clips on YouTube about the awesome acts of God and mass healing waves like Jesus did in the church. If you want to go there now, I'll wait as they are really interesting, not boring, but fun to watch. My favourite is John G Lake, one of God's generals. Here is a link you can look up.

God's Generals Series - Smith Wigglesworth:
https://www.youtube.com/watch?v=51_QnZtZhmc

Let's have a look at the 1950s. Jesus was very much the centre of the booming country of America. It was socially normal to go to church; if you didn't go to church, you were the odd one out. Prayer before dinners and giving thanks to Jesus was a custom. Even when eating out at restaurants, it was not unusual to give thanks before eating! Nowadays, you would be a very small minority!

Jesus was at the centre of most of society, and it was flourishing!

"Righteousness exalts a nation,

But sin is a reproach to any people" (Proverbs 14:34).

Tell that to any president or leader! It's the best wisdom you can get to get your country back on track! Thanks, Solomon and God!

Sure, there is not one country that doesn't have its share of sin, but how society either accepts the behaviors or opposes godlessness is how God can exalt a nation or cause it to to be a reproach.

Johnny Cash gave honor to Jesus, and in his later years wrote more songs about Jesus than ever! He came from spirituals, like Elvis Presley did. Elvis loved to sing spiritual songs, but they did not always get put on the networks! Check out Elvis giving thanks to God!

Elvis How Great Thou Art 1972:
https://www.youtube.com/watch?v=XlfcvUtUoOM

If you didn't know, the early blues were called spirituals! It started as singing about working on the cotton fields and how Jesus will help them overcome their slavery. Like anything that Hollywood has used for a profit, God blessed it to start with! So many famous musicians have come from the blues and even moden greats like John Mayer and Eric Clapton copied people like B.B. King. B.B. King said he started in church before he went to the army! The list will go on and on if we talk about how the music industry we love started from gospel music! Seriously, go find anyone and it will lead back to gospel music people who have been inspired, which will lead back to faith music.

American schools encouraged prayer in the 1950s; Australian schools too. Spiritual education was normal! Integrity from people's faith and the Bible promoted more integrity, which led to a different way of life in society.

It was rare for sports to be played on Sundays! Sunday was kept as a holy day of rest. Shops would shut and hotels would be closed! Families would have time together and embrace one another and go to church. Then they'd rest or have quiet time in the afternoon. There was more sense of local gatherings and mateship; more people had interactions and built lasting relationships with one another. People were more content to live next to each other for longer, not desiring bigger or better things then their fellow friends in their community. People would lift one another up and have working bees in neighborhoods and local helps! There were local dances that led to closer neighborhoods and more loyalty with one another! Jesus promotes peace and fulfillment in societies.

"I am the Lord your God,

Who teaches you to profit,

Who leads you by the way you should go.

Oh, that you had heeded My commandments!

Then your peace would have been like a river,

And your righteousness like the waves of the sea.

Your descendants also would have been like the sand,

And the offspring of your body like the grains of sand;

His name would not have been cut off

Nor destroyed from before Me" (Isaiah 48:17-19).

God is talking about Israel here, but the same can go for any other nation. God will not let the righteous be forsaken!

"The Lord will not allow the righteous soul to famish,
But He casts away the desire of the wicked" (Proverbs 10:3).

God loves to see justice and peace and happiness; He searches men's hearts and sees who are His!

Pete Seeger had a TV series that blended integrity and Jesus into mainstream society with modern musicians! Check out the legend John Hurt in the link below! Twenty minutes in on TV! We wouldn't have anything like that today!

Pete Seegers Rainbow Quest Hedy West, Mississippi John Hurt, Paul Cadwell Full Episode:
https://www.youtube.com/watch?v=Cd6lBQJAsEM&t=2371s

The 1950s era may have only been seventy years ago, but it might have been a couple of hundred in terms of society's lack of faith and the slow and steady decline of morals and desensitization of society! Even since the '90s, it has changed one-hundred fold. The pressures of life and quick pace of society have driven Jesus out of today's people's thoughts and minds! We are alway busy either with TV shows after work or desires to want more or to want better technology. We watch reviews on the latest gadgets, and it's so easy to be ensnared into traps to want for more and lust after more things that do not give lasting contentment. No wonder there is more depression in today's Gen Y / Z than ever before in history! So much false advertising of "happiness" and never reaching satisfaction or true values in society.

Check out the YouTube channel Thoughty2. He goes much more into why young people are affected by depression in the last forty years more than ever.

Why Young People Are More Depressed Than Ever Before:
https://www.youtube.com/watch?v=CPh8QoSdBPM

Look at Billy Graham: he was a pastor for fifty years and advised ten presidents! We need more godly men advising leaders in this world to direct them and guide them with godly wisdom and biblical understanding to help this world come into the blessings the Lord God wants to release to see His creation be blessed and not cursed!

If we compare the lifestyles of people today and the amount of tolerance there is in society toward sin, it's almost done a backflip! In fact, people are embracing sin and celebrating and encouraging it. It is even being enforced by politicians and even some churches. People can try to justify it with "well, we should go with the times; things change!" Yes, they sure do, but God doesn't change and His standards of evil certainly do not change just because we may be getting more "advanced," as every generation once thought!

"Jesus Christ is the same yesterday, today, and forever" (Hebrews 13:8).

Let's think about a music clip from 2020. If it was played back in the 1950s, it would have been considered xxx rated I'm not even joking!

The ratings for movies that were once considered for mature audiences back then are now acceptable to play to children. The 1950s cowboys and Indians in the outback with shooting and violence would be almost comical to viewers now! And what we would consider low to moderate ratings with sex, people hooking up with one night stands, and the general standards of humor would be considered crude and scandalous back then!

But as we feed those actions and watch people doing that, we then start to believe it's fine to start living like them. But that's not reality, and we don't see the heartache and depression that come with sin. For example, in today's society, men have never had more exposure to women and lusts. You can't walk down the street without seeing sex advertising. No wonder men are finding it hard to keep long relationships and they are burning in lust for other women on a daily basis. Men shouldn't be seeing perfect models, then when they get home to reality and daily life stresses, their partner isn't matching up to the looks or personality of some stars and their adventurous lifestyles from scripted movies or TV series. Men are becoming depressed! And that is only one side of the coin. What about girls/women seeing unattainable beauty from Photoshop and trying to emulate or reach that to be accepted in society? That can have devastating consequences on young girls and their health and confidence!

A lot of older generations say young people are weak these days. I say the opposite: young people have about ten thousand times the amount of issues in their environment to pull them down. The traps have been laid, and it's rare that young people will have the wisdom to be able to move around these issues without biblical wisdom and understanding. We are in a time when it's never been harder to start life: the demand and ruthlessness of business and cutthroat aspects of housing markets and wages! The scales have changed! When my dad was young, he bought his first house for eighteen thousand dollars in the suburbs, and he could pay that back within ten years with only one working in the household! Nowadays, it's more like fifteen to thirty-five years with two people working, depending on your jobs, studies, loans, lifestyle, and wages!

Life has never been so busy and chaotic and, to top it all off, less rewarding as it is in our society because it's always advertised in young people's faces that the reality we live will never be enough! No wonder there has been an increase in drugs and alcohol and suicides with the pressures of life and expectations set on our youth through our environments. The lustful lifestyle that is marketed to us can make us not be content and be a slave to our sinful natures. The Bible says this about our carnal flesh:

"Hell and Destruction are never full;
So the eyes of man are never satisfied" (Proverbs 27:20).

"Now godliness with contentment is great gain. For we brought nothing into this world, and it *is* certain we can carry nothing out. And having food and clothing, with these we shall be content. But those who desire to be rich fall into temptation and a snare, and into many foolish and harmful lusts which drown men in destruction and perdition. For the love of money is a root of all kinds of evil, for which some have strayed from the faith in their greediness, and pierced themselves through with many sorrows" (1 Timothy 6:6-11).

I am not saying we need to get back to the 1950s house prices and cowboys and Indians on TV; times change, investments grow, and interests change! We humans are very creative, thank goodness! But what I am saying is the slow decline in morals has led each generation after the next deeper into sin and less bothered by their consciences because of sins becoming accepted in society! When society puts up with sin, that can be called being an enabler of sin. If you give tacit consent, then behaviour will not change throughout generations! It doesn't mean you have to go out and tell everyone how to live holy: that does not work! No, not at all, but a better way is to change yourself and your morals to God's standard of a holy and live out a sancified lifestyle.

"Be holy, for I am holy" (1 Peter 1:16).

That can have an effect on people around you! And the ripple effect can then happen in society as more learn to love and have the knowledge to hate sin and love goodness. The more you grow in those, the more you will realize how a life of sin will never lead to anything good but only frustration and unhappiness in the long term and also in the short term.

After a wave of revival, there was a town founded in Illinois, **United States,** called Zion. They were so reformed and shaped and convicted by the Holy Spirit it changed society. Their town was booming with Christians and a different way of life. There was a church on every corner. They didn't even have doctors; they placed their faith in the living God who heals.

"If you diligently heed the voice of the Lord your God and do what is right in His sight, give ear to His commandments and keep all His statutes, I will put none of the diseases on you which I have brought on the Egyptians. For I am the Lord who heals you" (Exodus 15:26).

The Welsh Revival of 1904 changed the entire nation and led to hundreds of millions of people being saved and changing their lifestyles all around the world! It was reported that the miners' mules had to be restrained to listen to different commands because the miners were so convicted of their sin they would not use swear words to get the mules to move as they used to. The mules had to be retrained for commands in order to get the goods out of the mine! Police officers were out of jobs, and hotels and bars closed because society changed so much no one wanted to drink; instead, they wanted to go to church! The magistrates would wear white gloves because there were no crimes being committed! Now that is a change in society and a different way of life!

Here are some YouTube videos on various revivals:

The Welsh Revival of 1904:
https://www.youtube.com/watch?v=oJOu8eUhcys

God's Generals Series - Evan Roberts:
https://www.youtube.com/watch?v=8Jp85m6yl3s

The Azusa Street Revival (Documentary):
https://www.youtube.com/watch?v=HPtGJ35jIwA

God's Generals Series - John Alexander Dowie:
https://www.youtube.com/watch?v=3hXZ_1ZtHXQ

Check out Alexander Dowie's history and revivals that have taken place from this man's ministry. Although he did not end well, don't discount all the revivalists who were sparked by his ministry, John G lake included!

There is such rich church history of past revivals that simply have not made it into the history taught in school or universities. As the Bible says, "For the message of the cross is foolishness to those who are perishing" (1 Corinthians 1:18).

Clearly not all people who want to be educated are unsaved, but the standard of belief and school boards have determined what to teach. I can imagine there would be a lot more atheistic votes and the Christians would be a minority on these boards over the years. Naturally, it has occurred.

There seems to be a hush in society, and Jesus does not help one's reputation in being taken seriously. Society suppresses these truths because of our fallen nature, as we were reading before. There are actually dark forces rebelling against God and God's plan for mankind. Do you know the Bible says we are at enmity against God? And the wisdom of men is the foolishness of God. But more on that soon!

Did you know that in 1962-1963, America banned the Bible from their schools? Teenage pregnancies went up 553 percent and STDs rose 226 percent over the next twelve years, according to the YouTube clip of David Barton below. The education system's scores went down majorly! Before 1965, there were only 1,000 private Christian schools in America. Between 1974 and 1984, they increased to 32,000 Christian schools. Since 1963, violent crimes have increased 794 percent! You can check it out here: The Devastating Effects When Prayer Was Removed From School in America in 1962-63 - David Barton, https://www.youtube.com/watch?v=1No--GpdqCY. I mean the stats can go on and on, but that's not what this book is about!

Those changes happened over a short period of time! How much more polluted and more godless has society gotten now? Imagine what these new streaming sites can do to young adults or even young impressionable children. What about the future trickle down effect it might have!?

I once binged on streaming movies and series. I also loved to play many shooting games, and I became desensitised to the reality of sin without even knowing it! My nana or grandad or parents would sometimes come in and see what I was watching and comment on it and show their disapproval, but it was not all that bad in my opinion. As a young adult, I was conditioned to it, but to them, a violent punch that a hero did to a bad guy that would knock him through a wall was horrific since in the real world that could seriously cause fatal harm and murder! But not in movies, as they get straight back up and keep doing that for twenty minutes and still look nearly perfect! It's not reality we are putting into our minds, and I gave you a watered down version of some series and shows out there.

So what's my point with all these stats? People tend to judge themselves from each other's actions and acceptances, not necessarily coming from a just foundation, but a desensitised action or expression opposite to God's moral laws. That is how society's popular opinions are formed.

How much more with such interconnected platforms are we seeing more and more people conforming from endless hours of exposure? Young people have never ever had such influences with so much false advertising on happiness. There are many false images of people being happy and also jaded opinions to justify one's actions on who they are or what they call good, and guess what? If you oppose people's idealised ideas of morality and freedom, you become the minority in society for showing guidance in love for one's soul. It becomes attacked though the enmity of people's darkened thoughts toward God by the constant filling of content available to us 24/7. Welcome to political correctness where everything must be accepted besides God's truth, everyone has determined their own goodness valued on what they feel and see, and they follow one another's approvals of their own herd-minded morality!

"Woe to those who call **evil good,** and **good evil**;
Who put darkness for light, and light for darkness;
Who put bitter for sweet, and sweet for bitter!

"Woe to those who are wise in their own eyes,
And prudent in their own sight!" (Isaiah 5:20-21, emphasis added).

Remember some truths can be hard to follow because they may be in direct conflict with your lifestyle. That does not mean I will just pretend that there won't be a judgment! I love and care enough for you to tell you the truth even though it may appear I am attacking our very makeup of culture. To turn a blind eye would be foolish to do because God knows when your hours are up. You can't fool God and say, "I'll repent when I'm ninety on my deathbed." To have a plan like that will not work! Why would you risk eternity for some short-term pleasures that ultimately do not fulfill you?

"And some have compassion, making a distinction; but others save with fear, pulling them out of the fire, hating even the garment defiled by the flesh" (Jude 1:22-23).

Speaking about the early 1900s "original political correctness," or should I say, the Western world's political correctness, they considered themselves to be above others because of their colour! In the nineteenth century, slavery was considered normal and acceptable, but it's totally not acceptable now and with very good reason. Some things do change for the better. I'm not saying the community's underlying opinions are bad or all political correctness is bad, but if it does not have Jesus Christ as its foundation, it will become a false correctness and lead many people into sin and ultimately unhappiness.

It's normal for one to look at a questionable action, and if it is acceptable to others, it will slowly become the norm on a large scale. Welcome to paradigm shifts. Every generation has one, either big or small, but hopefully not the '80s with their awesome dress sense! Cough, cough! Hey, I ain't dissing it. It had to happen to get to the awesome '90s era that I'm from, of course!

So what is sin?
And why is sin bad?

The Bible says, "For the wages of sin is death" (Romans 6:23).

Sin in a nutshell is rebelling against God, and no matter how we judge ourselves in this society, acceptable norms are not how God will judge us. It's not according to our morals, but to His holiness if we do not repent of our sins.

Sin is bad because nothing good ever comes from it, and it leads to death, the second death. That is where hell is, where the fire is never quenched and the worm doesn't die. It's important to note that hell was not created for mankind, but for the angels that rebelled and if men and women rebel and reject the gospel of **love**.

We need to represent Jesus correctly by balancing love and the word of truth. Sure there are some Christians who do not represent Jesus Christ well; they are religious and even make hate signs and say horrible things to people about people. They are unbalanced in their approach, and I see them as an enemy toward God because they are not fulfilling His commandment to love one another. The world will see our love, not our hate! That never makes anyone come close to you, as it sets off defence mechanisms! The devil can cause false errors in the church to go out and make people feel uncomfortable and not want to get to know Jesus! They are not led by the Holy Spirit.

Jesus was gentle and meek, but He was very bold! He teaches people the correct way in love, and if they then choose not to follow Him, He does not force them to. He does warn that if you are found in your sins, there will ultimately be a judgment, but He pleads for a better way and He was sent to show the world that better way.

"Judge not, that you be not judged. For with what judgment you judge, you will be judged; and with the measure you use, it will be measured back to you" (Matthew 7:2).

You must be walking in the Holy Spirit and in love to be able to judge and to do so with wisdom and for the edifying of someone's soul, not the demise. Best be careful to not judge unless you are mature and in love or you may be judged according to your own words!

God will have no option but to judge because He is holy, and all injustice will meet a day to be made correct and justices will be made. That's a question many people have, but ultimately everything that has happened, good or bad, will get a reward or justice for what has taken place. Things will be made correct! So, we will get what we ask for. Sometimes we don't like it if we get judged for our own wrongdoings, but it's okay and just for others' judgments to be made when it suits us.

It's just and holy for Hitler to go to hell, right?

Yes, that's right because that is called justice; if he did not repent, then that is where he is!

What about rapists and murderers being convicted, that's justice, right? Yes, so hell can be viewed as justice for those who commit lawlessness. Hell is an appropriate thing for those who deserve it, right? Same with jails and our justice system. We don't say, "Ah, we shouldn't have punishment or consequences in our society. We can all do what we please!" Imagine then walking out of your house into the street! That is, if you still had a house left!

But it's unjust if *we* go to hell because we're not murderers or rapists or anything like that! But we do not know the **severity** of any sin! Sure, there are different sins, but all sin does lead to death if you are not found in Jesus Christ's new covenant, and there will be different judgments on the wickedness of your sin.

That's why Jesus is so awesome! He came to take away sin and stand before the Father and say, "I have paid his or her debt," so we can be free. This happens if we trust in Jesus and turn from our sins. We are not under the law that condemns now but under grace because all of us will still sin, but the difference of a repentant life is you will hate the sin you sometimes do!

The Bible says if we sin, we deserve hell. That is why everybody, rich or poor, famous or not, needs Jesus! The Bible says our own righteousness is as filthy rags; all the good we have done mixed with sin is like filth.

"But we are all like an unclean thing,
And all our righteousnesses are like filthy rags" (Isaiah 64:6).

"Having their own conscience seared with a hot iron" (1 Timothy 4:2).
   The Bible says that people's consciences can be seared, so what does that mean?

It means over time, morals can change as people dive deeper into sin. They will slowly become adaptive to their nature and be turned over to a reprobate mind as they have rejected the truth and replaced it with a lie. Are you still with me? I know nobody likes to be told how bad we are, but remember Jesus can be our righteousness for free! And we can experience God's best in life and in heaven. But let's learn a bit more because that's what this chapter is about.

I am shocked at how many Christians read every other content besides the Bible! The Bible seems to be replaced by huge genres of Christian books. Christians don't actually learn the truth from the main well that God intended us to learn from. The great preacher Charles Spurgeon once said that if his sermons ever stop you from getting into the Bible, you shouldn't listen to him or read his books! And I second that! Go read the Bible. I'm a mere man. I'd much rather know what God is saying, not offshoots from secondhand information, but from the Bible! The Holy Spirit who wrote the book knows the best way to reveal His manifold truths. If you really dig deep into the Bible, you will be surprised how many awesome things we can learn and the wisdom there is in God's love in the Old Testament and New Testament!

If you're not much of a reader like myself, I recommend the Word of Promise app with the New King James Version. It is by far the best with awesome narrations and high-quality voices to match each character perfectly, and you can binge listen! In a good way! But if you don't want to spend money on that in-app purchase, they do have the Gospel of John for free to listen to. That's all you need to get started. You will enjoy it!

So many people judge the Bible by its cover, but the old saying is, "Never judge a book by its cover!" And I might add, never judge a book by hearsay either, which can be from incorrect documentaries about Jesus made by people who don't know Him, nor want to know Him. There is so much incorrect information the history programs put out there about biblical history, from saying the Bible is not accurate or has contradictions to going as far as claiming Jesus had a wife and children! If you really want to, look into it with the whole counsel of God and with context! It will really show how wrong their information is. The Dead Sea Scrolls discovery shows how unchanged the Bible really is. As I said, it will unlock history to you in a greater way with the truth if you search for it.

As the very air you breathe exists, so it is. God is real, and He is for you and on your side! But first He wants to remove the sin from your life as a loving Father who corrects us. Why wouldn't God correct His children? God knows who are His, and so who He loves, He corrects!

"As far as the east is from the west,

So far has He removed our transgressions from us.

As a father pities his children,

So the Lord pities those who fear Him.

For He knows our frame;

He remembers that we are dust" (Psalm 103:12-14).

More on the love of God soon!

There is so much wisdom and gold in the Bible, yet it is so overlooked. People want to know formulas for money, trading, and the psychology of people, but they leave the true golden standard of life's questions unanswered. "Where is God?" a lot of people ask, but my answer is, Have you ever searched for Him? Or why He does not answer your prayers? Should He if you have rejected Him and only want to use Him when it's convenient for you?

Many people choose themselves over God, and they can become the god of themselves. They live the way they want to and do according to their lusts, and ultimately, it doesn't lead to fulfillment or satisfaction. You may think it does, but ultimately, it doesn't. We don't live forever! And one day we will all need Jesus. In saying that, God does answer many people's prayers in Jesus Christ's righteousness and in His grace if you really seek him and ask for forgiveness God will surely hear!

Here are a few links to videos about miracles from God:
Testifying about Jesus to the UN General Assembly - Lee Stoneking Miracle: https://www.youtube.com/watch?v=B1mDiGy2-0g&t=168s

Miracles of God caught on tape!!!: https://www.youtube.com/watch?v=_fkvKu2In98

Drug Addict Comes Face to Face with Jesus: https://www.youtube.com/watch?v=rbpET1SRrcs

Also, Pete Cabera Jr. is evangelising using the gifts of the Spirit and praying for people to be healed. Many more people are now making YouTube videos and doing online ministries because of Pete encouraging them to walk in the gifts Jesus has given to those to believe and change their paradigm about what type of world we really live in! Check out Tom Loud, who Pete inspired from his ministry too, but ultimately Jesus will get the honor for each healing as we are just vessels for his use!

"The effective, fervent prayer of a righteous man avails much" (James 5:16).

God is a very gracious God, and He does do things without you knowing. Have you ever felt not to go somewhere or to do something else at the last minute? Well, that could be God leading and directing your life for good and away from harm's way. Or He may even just want to bless you in maybe a job interview or bring a beloved pet into your life, which you may find brings joy into your life. God is the God of the big and the small. I like videos on YouTube that show the size of space then zoom back to earth. That really shows me we are just tiny, tiny people, like ants! The fact that He cares for us, even if we are not yet aware or mindful of Him, is awesome! And that He came down and died for us while we were still sinners is amazing. Anyway, back to what I was saying.

There are many answers in the book of Psalms as to why people struggle with prayer not being answered. That is a great study and a great way to learn to pray. It doesn't need to be overly complicated, as long as you mean it with all your heart, keep it simple, and you really want to desire to seek Him and His love. Watch God work in your life!

"Ask, and it will be given to you; seek and you will find; knock, and it will be opened to you. For everyone who asks receives, and he who seeks finds, and to him who knocks it will be opened. Or what man is there among you who, if his son asks for bread, will give him a stone? Or if he asks for a fish, will he give him a serpent? If you then, being evil, know how to give good gifts to your children, how much more will your Father who is in heaven give good things to those who ask Him! Therefore, <u>whatever you want men to do to you, do also to them, for this is the Law and the Prophets</u>" (Matthew 7:7-12, emphasis added).

The key to understanding in Psalms is that last verse, which is underlined for a reason. Treat others as you would want to be treated! That's the goodness of God's law that He wanted to teach us also to love and care for one another.

"For judgment is without mercy to the one who has shown no mercy. Mercy triumphs over judgment" (James 2:13).

But remember mercy does triumph over judgment. So, God prefers to show mercy before making a final judgment! God will always give people opportunities before judging as He is a righteous and merciful Judge.

Matthew 7:7 is a promise that He will reveal Himself to you if you ask. Give Him time to work out what's best for you in His timing, and in your dedication, you need to knock and seek. There's one thing God cannot do: He cannot lie.

"In hope of eternal life which God, who cannot lie" (Titus 1:2).

"Draw near to God and He will draw near to you" (James 4:8).

Although in our standard of what we think is good, also known as holy, we may be "good," in God's standard of good, we are not good. But God's goodness (Jesus!) makes us meet God's standard of good! That is the start of understanding why we need the goodness of Jesus imputed to us through putting our trust in Jesus to save us.

Ah, I'm glad I could type that rather than speak it!

CHAPTER 5
Why the crucifixion? And what is the good news?

Genesis 3:21 says, "Also for Adam and his wife the Lord God made tunics of **skin,** and **clothed** them" (emphasis added).

This was the first sacrifice God did to **cover** Adam and Eve. But it was more than just clothes as God had now seen that they had sinned and fallen from holiness. They were aware that they were naked and God locked them out of the garden of Eden.

God chose some sort of animal to show Adam and Eve that their sin had to be covered and that God needed to **cover mankind's sin** until His plan for the redemption of mankind was to be fulfilled.

This verse uses types and shadow.

For example, God made tunic skins for Adam and Eve and covered them, which is a very simple type and shadow of a few things that were to happen in the future . God provided a covering for Adam's and Eve's nakedness from sin, and the fact that it was made out of skin represents there was an animal sacrificed for them to be covered from their shame. That leads to Jesus's atonement—that God provided His son as a sacrifice for us! Just like Abraham and Isaac!

God uses these types and shadows for illustrations in the Bible. They are absolutely everywhere you look, and they all point to Jesus, the Holy Spirit, or the Father! Why does God use these types in His writings? Because He wants to give clear evidence of His plan and purposes, and He shows this to us as one way of His many ways to show His authorship on each Bible page. The Bible is very plain and clear, but also the Bible is very, very intricate to those who dig deep. There is more evidence of the Holy Spirit's fingerprint throughout many different authors; only the one true author, the Holy Spirit, would know how to incorporate them into His written word to be consistent and without fault! And only an overall picture can then reveal these details because we have the end result! Without the end result, no one would be able to see the hidden meanings and types the Holy Spirit is teaching!

What is a type? What is a shadow? It is about something that is! Think of it this way: A type is someone or something who God picks to display a story or a lesson that would ultimately point to the anti-type in the future. The anti-type is anti because it is not the type, but it is an anti-type that the type is leading to or revealing, get it? All the prophets in the Bible are types of Jesus, who was to come. All the stories and life lessons in the Bible and all the sacrifices from the Hebrews with the spotless lambs all lead to Jesus being the sinless lamb who came to take away the sins of the world.

And that it is a key point. I just said Jesus could "**take away,**" or remove, the sins of the world. The types could only "**cover**" the sins, like the tunics if you remember in Genesis 3:21, which is one of the first types or shadows in the Bible. That is the signature of the Holy Spirit's work that can define His personality in His writings using men, and it is one way we know that the Bible intertwines perfectly over thousands of years, even through many authors, about forty! The same Holy Spirit kept a consistent message, and that message always leads to Jesus, who was hidden until He was revealed to us by the Father. To have all sixty-six books written so consistently over thousands of years shows you the inspired work of the Holy Spirit. The odds that are fulfilled in having all those forty books line up perfectly without contradiction are quite impossible for our brains to understand. More than forty different authors have the same storyline and some without even knowing each other or having known all the past writings! That is the fingerprint of the Holy Spirit. Each page points to Jesus.

That's a great way to also discern genuine biblical books from other so-called "inspired" content that is left out of the Bible, such as the gnostic books. They do not have a focal point, and they rarely lead to Jesus. They are more on the "mysteries" of different aspects, which the Holy Spirit did not want us to know because it leads to error and doctrines of demons and the Nephilim. That's not helping mankind; it glorifies evil and not Jesus Christ and the saving work that is much needed in today's society. Ultimately, Jesus is the author of all ancient wisdom.

"I understand more than the ancients, Because I keep Your precepts" (Psalm 119:100).

If it's ancient wisdom you seek and the mysteries, then get to know Jesus and He will reveal all to you as you fully seek after Him.

As King David learned and talked about, there is more wisdom and knowledge in knowing Jesus and keeping His ways. King David wrote Scripture inspired by the Holy Spirit to teach us throughout the generations, keeping focus on Jesus, the author and finisher of our faith! I see the many authors of the Bible like light being refracted through a diamond into a rainbow. The key points came from the Holy Spirit but were refracted through the authors' personalities in their writings of the books of the Bible. Every detail matters, and God is in the details for a reason.

Understanding mysteries through relationship with Jesus.

As Paul, a New Testament apostle, said in the Bible for teaching, "And though I have the gift of prophecy, and understand **all mysteries** and all knowledge, and though I have all faith, so that I could remove mountains, but have not love, I am nothing. And though I bestow all my goods to feed the poor, and though I give my body to be burned, but have not love, it profits me nothing" (1 Corinthians 13:2-3, emphasis added).

"For assuredly, I say to you that many prophets and righteous men desired to see what you see, and did not see it, and to hear what you hear, and did not hear it" (Matthew 13:17).

That's Jesus saying to people when He was in His ministry how lucky they were to see God's wisdom and understanding! We have His very words: 783,137 words to be exact! With the KJV today, we can listen to the entire Bible in seventy-five hours! Do you know if you listened to the Bible for a little more than an hour at night for two months, you will have listened to the entire Bible? That's just one TV show less a night!

But I do recommend you start in the New Testament first, then go back to Genesis. You'll get a much bigger picture view having more context to unlock the Old Testament. There is much "meat" in all the books of the prophets, but first you must start with the milk! As babies need milk first, then are weaned off the milk to meat as they get a bit older and can chew and digest it much easier, so you can start with the New Testament and have more understanding to "digest" the Old Testament with.

I am not saying the Old Testament writings have more meat. The bible has milk and meat on every single page depending on the maturity of the reader, But for the mind of a new believer the New Testament certainly helps explain things in a way that is much easier to digest with context! The meat is really living and becoming like Jesus! And that is to know Love!

The cool thing about God's Word is you can have listened to it but only extracted one percent of its teachings. Think of it this way: Do race car drivers only do one lap when practicing? No! They keep going back for more laps so they get skilful in it. They produce better ways of getting quicker and better times as they get more experience and more confidence. They get to know the racetrack, how it operates, and how the car can react. The same is true with the Word of God: the more hunger you have, the more revelations God will give you to unlock His mysteries and His character of love on every page. Don't just pick a few sentences out of the Bible and then judge God off those so-called "contradictions" without context or understanding and don't judge His past judgments. Get to know God, and you will see exactly His love and kindness toward us!

Read Hebrews chapter 11 for many great stories in the Bible, and this chapter will give you great context for the other events in the Bible. Sure, some parts can be a bit slow, but you will learn to appreciate them later. Like fine wine or some jazz music, it takes time to develop or appreciate it with context!! Wine can taste better with time, and with context, jazz can be beautiful!

We are very lucky to have the Bible so readily available to us. Many people have been killed for their faith for carrying just a few pages of the Bible to others to read like the many prophets and people in the Hall of Faith!

We have sixty-six books of the Bible, and we have access to them at our fingertips! This has not always been the case. There have been wars against the false doctrines of the Roman Catholic empire for many years, and the popes and leaders of the Catholic Church did conspire to conduct their religion and have the Bible in a different language for many years. This was so they could not let the common people know what the Bible really said so as to control and manipulate the uneducated in fear and false doctrines for their own greed and control.

Ultimately, that led away from Jesus and the gospel, and it really shows where the error has crept in with that church. They have failed to be faithful ambassadors for Jesus but chose greed instead of the truth.

There are many instances where error has crept in. Usually, the aim of the devil is to attack the gospel of Jesus and the finished work of the cross and to lead people away. There are those feeling hurt from so-called Christians who are not really showing love and the fruit of that love through their own desires and needs. This selfishness ultimately leads to others being discouraged and hurt and can lead to people feeling betrayed by God!

Jesus is our high priest.

"That He might be a merciful and faithful High Priest in things pertaining to God" (Hebrews 2:17).

"For we do not have **a** High Priest who cannot sympathize with our weaknesses, but was in all points tempted as we are, yet without sin" (Hebrews 4:15, emphasis added).

The Catholic Church has fathers and priests, and they take the place of Jesus, who is our only mediator. Jesus is clearly our mediator and covering—not man, but faith in Jesus alone.

"For there is one God and one Mediator between God and men, the Man Christ Jesus" (1 Timothy 2:5).

We don't need a confession box that eliminates the need for Jesus as a mediator. We have access to the Father through Jesus, not a Catholic father who in centuries past took money for people's sins to be purged.

The devil is an imitator and a liar. He has been from the start, trying to be like God. He also tries to make God's church look bad and represent a false church to the world, and boy oh boy, how it has made the church look bad with the amount of false doctrine and their many sins ruining the lives of many poor victims. There is much to be stated about the wrong doctrine of that false establishment. If you're interested, check out **Mike Winger,** "Why I cannot be a Roman Catholic" on YouTube.

He is one teacher I highly recommend if you are a new or a seasoned Christian in the faith or even an atheist. He also defends the Christian faith with understanding and love to atheists with very logical responses.

Links for a full comprehensive study with Mike Winger on the Catholic Church:

Catholicism: Worth Arguing About (1st of 4 videos on Catholicism): https://www.youtube.com/watch?v=91n6erthX6A&list=PLZ3iRMLYFl HvsToYQdfDkiDE6dPkouIv3

Why Catholicism is WRONG: https://www.youtube.com/watch?v=TPG3vMeexks&t=45s

Roman Catholicism: Contending for the Faith: https://www.youtube.com/watch?v=7ZVHHmCOjOg

And I just want to point out something very clearly. I am not saying if you have been involved or are still involved with the Catholic Church that I am talking about you personally, but the establishment that has misled people in false ideas about Jesus. They worship Mary, Jesus's mother, more than Jesus, as if she is higher than Jesus. Another example that is not biblical is purgatory. You cannot buy someone out of purgatory because purgatory doesn't exist! It's not once mentioned in the Bible, which clearly states that:

"It is appointed for men to die once, but after this the judgment" (Hebrews 9:27).

There are many Reformation books and videos about church history. If you're interested in that type of stuff or want more understanding, please look into it for yourself as this could so easily go off topic.

If I have in any way hurt you if you're a Catholic, that's not my goal. My goal is to set you on the path to truth, and that is what ultimately sets people free. If you are in a Catholic Church, I'm not saying you're not saved, but there are about 1.2 billion confessing Catholics in the world, and I have met a lot of Catholic-confessing people who do not know the Bible or really much about Jesus! Like myself who was raised in a Christian house—we are Pentacostal—just because you're raised Christian doesn't make you one: I believed in Jesus, that He is real, but I did not know Him. For example, many people know of the president of the United States, but do they actually know him personally?

"You believe that there is one God. You do well. Even the demons believe—and tremble! But do you want to know, O foolish man, that faith without works is dead?" (James 2:19-20).

Let me tell you now that Jesus is more willing to know you and more eager to know you than you are to know Him because He loves and cares for you so much! But we can sometimes be too busy to want to know Him.

Questions are good, and you will find, if you question your Catholic Church, they will not be able to answer with the whole counsel of God and your questions will not be answered truthfully. I'm not saying the priest is lying to you, but he himself is misinformed or has chosen to believe a lie to accommodate his lifestyle. But in saying that, there are many <u>sincere priests</u> out there who have helped a lot of people and are good and faithful to Jesus, but some of their doctrine interpretations are without context and twisted to corporate agenda. The source that is taught to many is bad. If their foundation is not on solid ground and understanding of the Bible, there will naturally be more error mixed with truths, and that can open a wedge to all sorts of unbalanced teachings and can bring shame into the church.

Look at it this way: if you measure out a guideline for tiling a house's hallway all the way down, but you start just half a millimetre off the line and keep following the tiles laid before one another, at the end of the hallway, you will be off by a foot! It's amazing how allowing false concepts about the Bible can steer you straight into error. That's why it's so important that the Bible is to remain unchanged and not added to with extensions or embellishments from the pope's interpretation or "authority" to finalize ideas about doctrine, as the next pope can come along and be in error from the past as a tile following the past tile rather than the foundational line (Jesus) set for for us to learn from.

Now I want to state again the truth must not be hidden but let out to shine. This is in love and to save people from error and heartache! It's important to have discernment! I don't want to see 1.2 billion followers of the Catholic Church thinking it's all right to sin and their past sins can be purged by loved ones after they have died so they can live the way they want, then get someone to buy them out of purgatory if they did not want to follow Jesus and know His ways of righteousness and peace. It's fearful to think people can be misled about salvation and have an attitude of work mentality. No, you should **know** you are saved by His finished work! You should not be thinking, "If I only make it to purgatory (not that it exists), someone can intercede on my behalf after I have perished." Not all Catholic people live like that! But there is an overwhelming sense of Catholics having this mind-set of thinking they are saved but not really having known Jesus Christ and placing genuine repentance of sins and faith in a living relationship with Him. Your repentance will result in genuine faith, and the genuine faith will lead to the Lord's works on the earth for His glory.

Matthew 16:19 is what the Catholic Church builds their main doctrine of power on, claiming the pope has the keys and that the pope has the authority to forgive sins and change the Word of God. To keep this simple, let's move on. If you want to look into that for yourself, go to the Mike Winger series on Catholicism on YouTube. It's free, and we are all one in this body of Christ to edify and help one another grow spiritually.

"If you abide in My word, you are My disciples indeed. And you shall know the truth, and the truth shall make you free" (John 8:31-32).

"For I have not shunned to declare to you the whole counsel of God. Therefore take heed to yourselves and to all the flock, among which the Holy Spirit has made you overseers, to shepherd the church of God which He purchased with His own blood. For I know this, that after my departure savage wolves will come in among you, not sparing the flock. Also from among yourselves men will rise up, speaking perverse things, to draw away the disciples after themselves. Therefore, watch and remember that for three years I did not cease to warn everyone night and day **with tears**" (Acts 20:27-31, emphasis added).

"For the time will come when they will not endure sound doctrine, but according to their own <u>desires,</u> because they have itching ears, they will heap up for themselves teachers; and they will turn their ears away from the truth, and be turned aside to fables. But you be watchful in all things" (2 Timothy 4:3-5, emphasis added).

The same can go with this "prosperity" gospel and name it and claim it. It's garbage how some preachers have taken out of context biblical scriptures and spiritual laws and doctrines and have tried to apply the word of God to their own desires and wants and is not Jesus will. I am a Pentecostal too, and I see their errors. How many of those money preachers have ruined the lives of countless people by saying if you donate X amount, God will do this or God will do that? I am saddened, and it makes me want to cry that these people preaching a false gospel have tried to tarnish and blemish the truth. So unsaved people who are hurting do not want to listen to Christians, and I can understand why. They don't want to listen because of all the rubbish that is allowed on Christian networks.

We need a change: instead of Christians asking for money, let's give money away. Let us say, "Enough of this false gospel crap!" Let's learn to love people; let's put our itching ears away and follow the truth ...

"Most assuredly, I say to you, a servant is not greater than his master; nor is he who is sent greater than he who sent him" (John 13:16).

Jesus, the king of kings, was not in fancy private jets of the day, so to speak, or desiring the rich life. He was doing what His Father in heaven was asking Him to do; He was the suffering Messiah to save the world! Jesus was eating with sinners and the poor and needy. He was looked down on and judged and mocked. They sang songs about Him being a bastard and a drunk because of whom He had compassion on and His past with the virgin birth. He led the way to the needy and poor and showed them truth in love and care! He was teaching them better ways in life, and they were learning from His humility to do the right thing instead of doing the wrong thing.

"I have not come to call the righteous, but sinners, to repentance" (Luke 5:32).

Jesus went to the self-righteous, but they were right in their own eyes and would not, or could not, accept the truth because of their pride. Pride is like a blindfold; it stops people from seeing clearly because of their own will and deceitful heart.

"The heart is deceitful above all things,
And desperately wicked" (Jeremiah 17:9).

Yes, God has different ministries for different needs, but you will see their **fruit** if they are Jesus's disciples.

"Beware of false prophets, who come to you in sheep's clothing, but inwardly they are ravenous wolves. You will know them by their **fruits.** Do men gather grapes from thornbushes or figs from thistles? Even so, every good tree bears good fruit, but a bad tree bears bad fruit. A good tree cannot bear bad fruit, nor can a bad tree bear good fruit. Every tree that does not bear good fruit is cut down and thrown into the fire. Therefore, by their fruits you will know them" (Matthew 7:15-20, emphasis added).

Paul uses fruit as an example in the Bible as a way we can understand that our actions can be good or bad. See Galatians 5:16-25.

You will be able to see if someone cares by their actions or lack of actions, and you will determine if their fruit is good or they show their true actions with their mouth only. As Jesus says, the mouth is where the heart reveals its truths.

"Either make the tree good and its fruit good, or else make the tree bad and its fruit bad; for a tree is known by its fruit. Brood of vipers! How can you, being evil, speak good things? For out of the abundance of the heart the mouth speaks. A good man out of the good treasure of his heart brings forth good things, and an evil man out of the evil treasure brings forth evil things. But I say to you that for every idle word men may speak, they will give account of it on the day of judgment. For by your words you will be justified, and by your words you will be condemned" (Matthew 12:33-37).

Ok, so why was Jesus explaining about all of that necessary?

"Have no fellowship with the unfruitful works of darkness" (Ephesians 5:11).

Well, it's important to expose the false doctrines that lead to unfruitful living. Many people say a prayer and then say, "It's ok to sin, and I can go confess it, and then if I don't, someone can always buy my way into heaven." It leads to a self-destructive lifestyle that allows people to have itching ears for false doctrines for excuses in their lifestyle. They think they're saved by a false gospel but the tree is not producing good fruit but bad fruit to put it simply a bad fruit tree cannot produce good fruit nor a good fruit tree produce bad fruit it is the identity that Jesus is talking about not that our good fruit saves us but if we are saved by grace our new man and its identity being good will want to produce good fruit for Jesus and if we are not saved we do not have the understanding or love of Jesus is our life's and to the unsaved will live from their old man and its fallen nature that has not changed and that will only produce bad fruit. And it's very sad to see someone with a false sense of security They think they are in fact in the faith of Jesus, but they do not KNOW Him **personally as lord and saviour and not letting the Holy Spirit purify them by is sanctifying them by the word of God or letting grace have its perfect work in their life's.**

It's important to understand this is done in **love,** not in hate. It's a **warning** for people who are simply not taught correct doctrine that can lead them into error, and it could possibly be an error that leads into a Christless eternity because of a lack of diligence to know the truth.

"Not everyone who says to Me, 'Lord, Lord,' shall enter the kingdom of heaven, but he who does the will of My Father in heaven. Many will say to Me in that day, 'Lord, Lord, have we not prophesied in Your name, cast out demons in Your name, and done many wonders in Your name?' And then I will declare to them, 'I never knew you; depart from Me, you who practice lawlessness!'" (Matthew 7:21-23).

The gospel is not an excuse to get away with sin. The gospel is there for love and for God to show grace, not for it to be used as a licence to sin.

Now I am not promoting good works to get you to heaven as it is heavily overstated in some circles, but to put it simply: If you are born again of the **Spirit,** remember that as you know the truth, you will be very glad that your past life of sin has been washed away. You will become a good tree with good fruit naturally, and good fruit will be produced in love! Now am I saying that once we are saved, we are perfect and we can't sin? No, we all sin, but we live in God's grace and his favour helps us grow even though we may sin his love helps us get back up again to continue in his will for our life! Grace empowers growth! Without grace we would easily become discouraged in our Christian walk.

"What shall we say then? Shall we continue in sin that grace may abound? Certainly not! How shall we who died to sin live any longer in it?" (Romans 6:1).

We are to take our cross and follow Jesus, and if we follow Him in His death, we are then raised in life at the end of the age like He was. To follow Him in His death means to die to one's sinful nature and follow the Father's will for our lives. But back to sin: we all sin, and we cannot not sin because of our fallen nature! This may make sense to you if you read it slowly! The Bible says we are still capable of sinning, but it's not our new nature that Jesus has given that sins. But our old nature can sometimes try and control us, but with the Holy Spirit's power, He keeps us from wanting to sin and teaches us to hate the sin lest it become very sinful!

Apostle Paul says, "For what I am doing, I do not understand. For what I will to do, that I do not practice; but what I hate, that I do. If, then, I do what I will not to do, I agree with the law that it is good. But now, it is no longer I who do it, but sin that dwells in me. For I know that in me (that is, in my flesh) nothing good dwells; for to will is present with me, but how to perform what is good I do not find. For the good that I will to do, I do not do; but the evil I will not to do, that I practice. Now if I do what I will not to do, it is no longer I who do it, but sin that dwells in me" (Romans 7:15-20, emphasis added).

False gospel?

I marvel that you are turning away so soon from Him who called you in the grace of Christ, to a different gospel, which is not another; but there are some who trouble you and want to pervert the gospel of Christ. But even if we, or an angel from heaven, preach any other gospel to you than what we have preached to you, let him be accursed. (Galatians 1:6-8)

There is **the Gospel,** and there is a false gospel. What gospel are you being taught? If I am to teach you the gospel, I want to highlight for you that the gospel I am **not teaching** is the "do as you please" gospel, but rather I want to teach you the real gospel that leads to eternal peace and joy with the King of Kings, Jesus Christ, who is love. Mockery of Him will not be tolerated, and the gospel cannot be diluted down with the "suit your own needs" teachings. The gospel is called the good news to you: if you allow God in your life, you will come to understand that the gospel and all its truths will give you a peace and love in your heart. That is the good news, that Jesus can take every burden from you and help you to be your very best in life. Sometimes that's suffering for the gospel's sake, or sometimes that's living a free and joyous life in the Lord if you put to death your old self, but remember, it is ultimately about your eternity, as that is what matters.

What is one thousand years or one hundred years compared to an infinite amount of years that never end in eternity? That is why you really want to make your decision now to be happy in those endless digits, not the small ones here, although Jesus will give you joy and strength to live in a world that is under the sway of the evil one until the devil's time comes to be sent to hell.

"The peace of God, which surpasses all understanding, will guard your hearts and minds through Christ Jesus" (Philippians 4:7).

"We know that we are of God, and the whole world lies under the sway of the wicked one" (1 John 5:19).

"And fire came down from God out of heaven and devoured them. The devil, who deceived them, was cast into the lake of fire and brimstone where the beast and the false prophet are. And they will be tormented day and night forever and ever" (Revelation 20:10).

Why did we need a sacrifice?

Why we needed a sacrifice was to **remove** our sins so we could become the righteousness of Jesus Himself. The Father chose to do that by displaying Him on the cross and the sin of mankind was nailed to the cross. Since Jesus lived a blameless and sinless life, He conquered death that had entered into the world through Adam. Since Jesus obeyed righteousness, death had no power over Him.

"So when this corruptible has put on incorruption, and this mortal has put on immortality, then shall be brought to pass the saying that is written: 'Death is swallowed up in victory.'
'O Death, where is your sting?
O Hades, where is your victory?'

The sting of death is sin, and the strength of sin is the law. But thanks be to God, who gives us the victory through our Lord Jesus Christ" (1 Corinthians 15:54-57).

And since death had no dominion over Jesus because He did not sin but obeyed the 613 commandments, it had no legal right over Him when He died on the cross.

When it was time, the Holy Spirit that was with Jesus quickened/healed His mortal body and He rose from the dead and took captivity captive.

"'When He ascended on high,
He led captivity captive,
And gave gifts to men.'
"(Now this, 'He ascended'—what does it mean but that He also first descended into the lower parts of the earth? He who descended is also the One who ascended far above all the heavens, that He might fill all things.)" (Ephesians 4:8-10).

"Putting off the body of the sins of the flesh, by the circumcision of Christ, buried with Him in baptism, in which you also were raised with Him through faith in the working of God, who raised Him from the dead. And you, being dead in your trespasses and the uncircumcision of your flesh, He has made alive together with Him, having forgiven you all trespasses, having wiped out the handwriting of requirements that was against us, which was contrary to us. And He has taken it out of the way, having nailed it to the cross. Having disarmed principalities and powers, He made a public spectacle of them, triumphing over them in it" (Colossians 2:11-15).

Sometimes doctor visits are not pleasant, but they're important to pinpoint the issue and correct it before it can lead to harm. We need to do that with sin for your spiritual well-being; simply ignoring it will not fix the issues of life. Accepting Jesus is the only way out of this journey to ultimately peace, happiness, and joy forever more without sin when God makes all things new!

That is why we are in such need of Jesus and how much He loves us: He went to the most painful and slow execution for us. Check out facts about the crucifixion on YouTube if you want to get an awe for Jesus and His act of love for humankind.

The Crucifixion | A Medical Perspective:
https://www.youtube.com/watch?v=T-EVfxABSoU

Why is His blood so important?

"For it is the life of all flesh. Its blood sustains its life" (Leviticus 17:14).

The way God made life is in our blood, and our blood is our life source. Without blood in our bodies, nothing would have life! It sustains life. Since our blood has been corrupted through our sin, we needed Jesus Christ, born of a virgin, who was not tainted with sin, but He was holy from God to take away our sins legally.

That is why Jesus needed to die for His blood to be an offering and to seal His New Testament with a new and better covenant, no longer under the 613 laws, but Jesus fulfilled those laws. Remember how we were talking about the laws God set with Moses? We were under the law! Or the law of our conscience.

But now there's a better promise to those who believe and are not under the law and the judgment of God, but we are now under the grace of God because Jesus fulfilled the law for us.

Now we can enter into the promises God has given us. If you believe that Jesus came and died and rose on the third day, you will be saved and you are now in Jesus. Through one man, sin entered into the world. You can have faith in Jesus and be in His spiritual body of covering. Here is Romans 8:1-17, which explains the redemption of one's soul through the victory of the cross and sin:

(Romans 8: 1-17 ESV)
"There is therefore now no condemnation for those who are in Christ Jesus. For the law of the Spirit of life has set you free in Christ Jesus from the law of sin and death. For God has done what the law, weakened by the flesh, could not do. By sending his own Son in the likeness of sinful flesh and for sin, he condemned sin in the flesh, in order that the righteous requirement of the law might be fulfilled in us, who walk not according to the flesh but according to the Spirit. For those who live according to the flesh set their minds on the things of the flesh, but those who live according to the Spirit set their minds on the things of the Spirit. For to set the mind on the flesh is death, but to set the mind on the Spirit is life

and peace. For the mind that is set on the flesh is hostile to God, for it does not submit to God's law; indeed, it cannot. Those who are in the flesh cannot please God. You, however, are not in the flesh but in the Spirit, if in fact the Spirit of God dwells in you. Anyone who does not have the Spirit of Christ does not belong to him. But if Christ is in you, although the body is dead because of sin, the Spirit is life because of righteousness. If the Spirit of him who raised Jesus from the dead dwells in you, he who raised Christ Jesus from the dead will also give life to your mortal bodies through his Spirit who dwells in you.

So then, brothers, we are debtors, not to the flesh, to live according to the flesh. For if you live according to the flesh you will die, but if by the Spirit you put to death the deeds of the body, you will live. For all who are led by the Spirit of God are sons of God. For you did not receive the spirit of slavery to fall back into fear, but you have received the Spirit of adoption as sons, by whom we cry, "Abba! Father!" The Spirit himself bears witness with our spirit that we are children of God, and if children, then heirs-- heirs of God and fellow heirs with Christ, provided we suffer with him in order that we may also be glorified with him."

What Paul is saying in the Bible is basically this: If you are in Jesus Christ in faith of what Jesus did for you and you also now die to your old passions and carnal attitudes toward God, it will allow the Holy Spirit in your life to come and transform you into a new being. He will change your actions and your life for good, not bad, and you will be free from any condemnation forever if you seek forgiveness in Jesus. You will grow with Him and He will gently teach you your faults and you will learn to love, and to love is to fulfill the New Testament covenant. The new covenant is this, in short: eternal life and blessing, freedom and joy in a new world Jesus will create once this world has run its course and all things have been fulfilled.

Read Revelation, the end book in the Bible, for the full understanding of the promise. It might sound funny, but I highly recommend Revelation for new believers or people who want to know Jesus. There are some things you may not understand without the bigger picture, but there are some awesome things in there to give you a spark and hunger for the rest of the book. As I said before, start with Revelation or the four Gospels (Matthew, Mark, Luke and John), and then go through the New Testament to

Revelation. Genesis is the start of the Bible. Romans is great too, about the inner workings of the cross as we have briefly gone over.

Remember at the start of the book I said people use Jesus's name in vain as a swear word. That is why: because of our fallen nature. Romans says, "Because the carnal mind is enmity against God" (8:7). Enmity, what does that mean? It means an active and mutual hatred or ill will toward one's being. I'm not saying you hate God, but it is in our flesh to have a tendency to be against Him in our fleshly nature. I hope it's starting to make sense why this world is naturally against God in every area! That is why, because of our fallen nature, we tend to be against God without knowing it. Well, we do really know, but we suggest to ourselves we are more correct than our Maker, but in His love, He knew that about us but yet still came and did what He did for us so we can be united with Him again! He really sees the bigger picture!

Why did He need to die?

"For where there is a testament, there must also of necessity be the death of the testator. For a testament is in force after men are dead, since it has no power at all while the testator lives. Therefore not even the first covenant was dedicated without blood. For when Moses had spoken every precept to all the people according to the law, he took the blood of calves and goats, with water, scarlet wool, and hyssop, and sprinkled both the book itself and all the people, saying, 'This is the blood of the covenant which God has commanded you.' Then likewise he sprinkled with blood both the tabernacle and all the vessels of the ministry. And according to the law almost all things are purified with blood, and without shedding of blood there is no remission" (Hebrews 9:16-22).

"In that He says, 'A new covenant.' He has made the first obsolete. Now what is becoming obsolete and growing old is ready to vanish away" (Hebrews 8:13).

Okay, so now the hard stuff has been dealt with—sort of! A few more ideas how we all fit together as God's family are coming next. There's just four chapters left. Keep going! We are nearly coming to the best part, God's love! But first let's ask this question in the next chapter!

CHAPTER 6
Why is the church needed?

The church is needed for evangelism! And many other reasons! But the main reason is it will be needed throughout the generations until Christ returns to take back His church, who is His holy and spotless bride, home to live in peace.

You may be wondering, How do you mean bride? The church has been described in Revelation as His bride, and other Old Testament prophets have prophesied this same thing.

"'Lord God Omnipotent reigns! Let us be glad and rejoice and give Him glory, for the marriage of the Lamb has come, and His wife has made herself ready.' And to her it was granted to be arrayed in fine linen, clean and bright, for the fine linen is the righteous acts of the saints" (Revelation 19:6-8).

"Through their [the Hebrews'] fall, to provoke them to jealousy, salvation has come to the Gentiles. Now if their fall is riches for the world, and their failure riches for the Gentiles, how much more their fullness!

"For I speak to you Gentiles; inasmuch as I am an apostle to the Gentiles, I magnify my ministry, if by any means I may provoke to jealousy those who are my flesh and save some of them. For if their being cast away is the reconciling of the world, what will their acceptance be but life from the dead?

"For if the firstfruit is holy, the lump is also holy; and if the root is holy, so are the branches. And if some of the branches were broken off, and you, being a wild olive tree, were grafted in among them, and with them became a partaker of the root and fatness of the olive tree, do not boast against the branches" (Romans 11:11-18).

The Hebrews are the natural branches in the olive tree, but since they mostly rejected Jesus, the good news of the gospel has gone out to the entire world to allow non-Hebrews to become a wild branch grafted in. We can all partake in God's fullness that He has for those who love Him.

But Paul is saying that if and when the Hebrew people come back and repentant and believe that Jesus is in-fact messiah, they will be able to be grafted back in and they will flourish very well as it's natural for them to be a part of the olive tree, aka Jesus!

"The wedding is ready, but those who were invited were not worthy. Therefore go into the highways, and as many as you find, invite to the wedding" (Matthew 22:8-9).

You see, God wants to invite everybody to become heirs of Abraham and to be called the sons of God! That is the church's main mission: to spread the good news before His mercy is not found and the time of grace has finished and He is ready for judgment and all wrongs to be made right. Those who are in Jesus Christ have their sins remembered no more!

"'Come now, and let us <u>reason together</u>,'

Says the Lord,

'Though your sins are like scarlet,

They shall be as white as snow;

Though they are red like crimson,

They shall be as wool'" (Isaiah 1:18, emphasis added).

Again for clarity, there is no replacement of the Hebrews.

The church is made up of His people who have been added onto the natural branch of the Hebrew people. Since the Hebrews mostly rejected Jesus's first coming, Jesus made it possible for the Gentiles (non-Hebrew people) to enter into the promises that He gave Abraham's seed (he was the first Hebrew). Now having a look at Abraham, remember how I said that there is a natural seed of Abraham and also a spiritual seed? Well, it turns out that to be the seed of Abraham is not just being physically related to him, but we can be adopted into his family and can now be called sons of God. The seed of Abraham in the spiritual sense, apart from the Hebrew people also being welcomed into the spiritual seed through Christ, are circumcised in heart as a Hebrew and will flourish beyond measure in Jesus as much as a natural branch!

"Now to Abraham and his seed were the promises made. He does not say, 'And to seeds,' as of many, but as of one, 'And to your Seed,' who is Christ. And this I say, that the law, which was four hundred and thirty years later, cannot annul the covenant that was confirmed before by God in Christ, that it should make the promise of no effect. For if the inheritance is of the law, it is no longer of promise; but God gave it to Abraham by promise" (Galatians 3:16).

"Blessed be the God and Father of our Lord Jesus Christ, who has blessed us with every spiritual blessing in the heavenly places in Christ, just as He chose us in Him before the foundation of the world, that we should be holy and without blame before Him in love, having predestined us to adoption as sons by Jesus Christ to Himself, according to the good pleasure of His will, to the praise of the glory of His grace, by which He made us accepted in the Beloved.

"In Him we have redemption through His blood, the forgiveness of sins, according to the riches of His grace which He made to abound toward us in all wisdom and prudence, having made known to us the mystery of His will, according to His good pleasure which He purposed in Himself, that in the dispensation of the fullness of the times He might gather together in one all things in Christ, both which are in heaven and which are on earth— in Him. In Him also we have obtained an inheritance, being predestined according to the purpose of Him who works all things according to the counsel of His will, that we who first trusted in Christ should be to the praise of His glory.

"In Him you also trusted, after you heard the word of truth, the gospel of your salvation; in whom also, having believed, you were sealed with the Holy Spirit of promise, who is the guarantee of our inheritance until the redemption of the purchased possession, to the praise of His glory" (Ephesians 1:3-14).

I hope this is giving you a clearer picture of how God has set salvation up for the world and that He has a plan for every one of us! But to keep this book short, we will not go into that here!

CHAPTER 7
The love of God.

For this chapter, if you don't mind, I want to take Bible verses out of the Old Testament and the New Testament and just get you to read His words and His acts of love. I will be completely honest with you: many do not like the Old Testament. If you scan over it quickly, I can understand there is a lot of judgment in there. But if you really go in depth, there is more love in the Old Testament than the New Testament. Despite how the people of Israel defied God and chose to do crazy things against Him, He was so patient and loving to His people, and He gave so many reasons and options for repentance for the people of Israel. Throughout history, the Hebrews would go through prosperity and then fall from God and trust in their own ways and do evil acts. They played the harlot with God and were unfaithful to Him, but God kept caring and continued His love for the Hebrews, but He still isn't done yet! He still plans to save them, as they are the apple of His eye. There is no replacement for Israel; the church is very much in accordance with His plans for Israel to all be one.

We can see in the Bible the acts of love God has shown mankind, and we can get to know the love of God better from reading His Word and understanding His ways. We can all learn to apply the knowledge that God has revealed in His Word.

"Love suffers long and is kind; love does not envy; love does not parade itself, is not puffed up; does not behave rudely, does not seek its own, is not provoked, thinks no evil; does not rejoice in iniquity, but rejoices in the truth; bears all things, believes all things, hopes all things, endures all things.

"Love never fails" (1 Corinthians 13:4-8).

If we look at Jesus and His ministry, He showed the example of how to be love! Jesus would walk miles to towns to preach the gospel of love. He walked for miles to heal people and show them a better way in life. He ate with the poor and needy; He showed the outcasts of society love and showed them hope in life!

God is love

As humans, we can let our experiences, good or bad, lead us to believe certain aspects of life and shape how we understand foundational truths that we believe. For example, there are many aspects of love but what aspect of love do you understand and know?

The Bible says in (1 John 4:8: ESV) "Anyone who does not love does not know God, because God is love".

Let's have a look at the characteristics of our love, and then let's take our knowledge of what we understand to be love and compare it to biblical love Jesus shows to us.

Often we like to be around people in our lives because of the joy and pleasure people can give into our lives. We can make relationships and grow with love for one another, but say there is a particular person around you who you don't really like or get along with. Do you love that person?

Now I'm not speaking about family because you sort of have to love them no matter what they do because they are of your blood, so it makes it a different type of love!

To put it bluntly, we love what is our own. We don't love other people's kids; we show favour to our own kids first. It's just the way it is: we love what is ours because we love ourselves first. Now is that the kind of love God shows?

"If you love those who love you, what benefit is that to you? For even sinners love those who love them. And if you do good to those who do good to you, what benefit is that to you? For even sinners do the same. And if you lend to those from whom you expect to receive, what credit is that to you? Even sinners lend to sinners, to get back the same amount. But love your enemies, and do good, and lend, expecting nothing in return, and your reward will be great, and you will be sons of the Most High, for he is kind to the ungrateful and the evil. Be merciful, even as your Father is merciful"(Luke 6:32-36 ESV).

Jesus demonstrated His love toward us when we did not want to know Him or even hated Him.

"For one will scarcely die for a righteous person--though perhaps for a good person one would dare even to die--but God shows his love for us in that while we were still sinners, Christ died for us. Since, therefore, we have now been justified by his blood, much more shall we be saved by him from the wrath of God.For if while we were enemies we were reconciled to God by the death of his Son, much more, now that we are reconciled, shall we be saved by his life.More than that, we also rejoice in God through our Lord Jesus Christ, through whom we have now received reconciliation"

(Romans 5:7-11 ESV).

So we can sometimes see love very differently than Jesus. We see love as: if you do this, I'll love, or I love you because you are beautiful or handsome, or I love you because you provide for me and you have a good Job, or you are skillful and funny!

But I want to show you a love where Jesus loves you not because of what you can do for Him, but He loves because He sees you and wants the very best for you. Even though you have been in rebellion toward Him and you have sinned, He sees your faults and all your secret intents and your past, He knows your weaknesses, He knows it all! But yet He chooses to love you. I wonder how many people would truly love us if people knew all our thoughts. It would be very hard!

Jesus's very nature is love. I want to get into a little bit of Greek language. But you may ask, Why Greek?

Two reasons: One, Greek was used as a main source for the Bible we know today!
And the original Hebrew books that we know as the Old Testament writings were converted into a Greek book called the Septuagint. Around seventy scholars around 285 BC converted the original text into Greek, and most likely that is the book Jesus used!

The Greek language is very unique because it is so expressive! There are many ways to describe something. It is very,very accurate, if not more expressive than the Hebrew language, as you will soon find out with the list of different loves the Greeks used in daily life! For us English speakers, we may say I love my wife or I love pizza, but do you really love your pizza as much as you love your wife? No! Well, I hope not!

Having understanding about biblical text that was written in Greek is very informative when it comes to the way God wants us to understand His Word so it is very hard for His truth to be manipulated into wrong wordings as many people try. But for those who really seek and want to understand the truth, the Greek language is the best for keeping context! But let's stick to how He was showing different types of love!

The New Testament was written in Greek too. In the time period, Greek was the standard global language, like how English is today.

I'll keep this short, but it's good to understand how we can view love and how it's important not to misplace our understanding of what we perceive love to be and that we don't dismiss godly love for our many types of love.

Sometimes we can let our experiences of love let us down when it comes to God because the love of our parents or relationships can leave those hurts, and we can think God loves or uses us the same! But let's look deeper into the many different loves in the Greek language, then let's look at what Jesus is teaching in His wording for love.

- Eros (romantic, passionate love)

Known as a sexual love or lust.

- Ludus (playful love)

Or what we would know as flirting with one another as a young love

- Storge (familiar love)

Known as between family members, a protective kinship-based love

- Mania (obsessive love)

One we often hear this term in English in songs or games, but it means obsession or extreme jealousy.

- Philia (affectionate love)

Known as without physical attraction, *platonic,* or friendship love or brotherly love, like with David and Jonathan in the Bible.

- Pragma (enduring love)

Is known as commitment or understanding long-term best interests.

• Philautia (self love)

We must look after ourselves before we can look after others; we must love our own flesh and care for it.

But the main love I want to add is one that is widely expressed in the Bible but very, very rarely used in the Greek language or writings:

• **Agape (selfless, universal love)**

Source;
https://greekcitytimes.com/2020/02/14/the-8-ancient-greek-words-for-love/

That is the love Jesus was teaching His disciples: to be selfless! That is the highest form of love, and agape really came back to life in Jesus's time and shortly after the Bible because of His character and love He showed for people. He was selfless and cared for others before Himself; He really showed a pure form of love that we can understand.

That is the love I want to introduce to you, and for us Christians, that is the love we should be showing the world.

"A new commandment I give to you, that you love one another: just as I have loved you, you also are to love one another.By this all people will know that you are my disciples, if you have love for one another." (John 13:34-35, ESV).

Jesus did not come for the righteous, but He came for the poor and needy. He came to show hope and to give honor. He came to show love and that there is no partiality in His standards. No matter who you are, Jesus will want to show you agape love if you let Him and accept His free gift of love. He said in the Bible He has not come to judge the world, but He has come to save the world! He does say those who do not believe are judged already because they choose to be prideful and go on their own righteousness.

I hope we can have the humility to say, "I am but a mere human being and my knowledge only can go so far. I won't let my lack of understanding or lack of knowledge get in the way of a bigger and better plan Jesus wants to show me, even though I may not understand why some things can happen in this world."

But I leave that with the Father. Sometimes one of the best ways the enemy can try to defeat evangelism and to get people to turn people's hearts away from God is to say, If God is so good why do bad things happen? I think I have tried to explain to you by now why this can happen because of our choices and the free will that God has given us and we have chosen to go down the wrong path with sin. The Bible says those who hate me love death. Jesus Christ is life, and if we want to reject Him, He will give us over to our wishes, but that means the second death.

There is a day when all things in this world, all injustices, will be made right at the great white throne of judgment (see Revelation 20).

"...not knowing that the goodness of God leads you to repentance?" (Romans 2:4)

Now sometimes we can be victims of circumstances too not every result of our sin is why bad things happen is not always our fault, but it can be from other people's bad decisions to let sin reign that can affect everybody or accidents that may naturally occur.

In God's wisdom, He has chosen to allow evil to exist for a very short period of time compared to eternity. And He has chosen not to deal with sin straight away, but He has chosen to make all things right at the end of the age for our sakes! He sees the bigger picture just like some scientists believe we are in a line of time and God is outside of that line of time.

Just as a river flows, He is above and He can see where the river leads and He can direct its path (time) by molding its direction (our actions) for the best possible outcome. So don't let your understanding see only the negative around you because I'm sure there is more good that you cannot see Him doing!

"The righteous man perishes, and no one lays it to heart; devout men are taken away, while no one understands. For the righteous man is taken away from calamity; he enters into peace"

(Isaiah 57:1-2 ESV)

The Bible says seek him while He is found see (Isaiah 55-6), and the more you're around Christian environments, the more you will see God acting in your midst! You can't expect to see and experience God in action if you have never had any interest in wanting to find out. If you ever go to a Spirit-filled church, soon you will see God working! Just like Gods Generals and some of the YouTube links search and you will find!

It would be like judging a sport player without seeing him/her in action! For example, if you don't know of a sport and you don't watch it or want to find anything out about it, you won't know what's going on. But if you're involved and you see the games and you watch the sport, you can come to understand that there's active action you were never aware of.

God can work the very same way in your life as you want to seek Him and get involved. If you want to seek and search after Him with discernment, the Holy Spirit can lead you into all truths.

His goodness is everywhere, even His love is in nature. Look at the peaceful environments He has created in the world to thrive. Look at just a glimpse of His personality in creating that harmony and beauty in our fallen world! Imagine it without sin—well, that's what He is planning for us! Get excited and believe because it is a reality as much as we enjoy this one!

There are also rewards that Christians can receive. The Bible talks about many crowns to those who compete and want to share the gospel and help share God's love. He not only forgives us and makes us a part of His kingly inheritance, but then He gives us honor and places us with Him in heaven to serve Him and be faithful to Him. He will give us rewards and titles in heaven!

"I have fought the good fight, I have finished the race, I have kept the faith. Henceforth there is laid up for me the crown of righteousness, which the Lord, the righteous judge, will award to me on that Day, and not only to me but also to all who have loved his appearing."(2 Timothy 4:7-8 ESV).

"and raised us up with him and seated us with him in the heavenly places in Christ Jesus, so that in the coming ages he might show the immeasurable riches of his grace in kindness toward us in Christ Jesus"(Ephesians 2:6-7 ESV).

Don't listen to lies

If you feel you cannot be forgiven, trust me: that is a lie. Many people believe the lies from the devil that they can't be forgiven. Jesus's blood is worth every single drop, and He wants to use His sacrifice of love to cover your sins and give you hope and an expected end!

Don't let the enemy try to lie to you and try to put on horse blinkers as to where they want to direct your attention. God's love is the doorway and the only way to experience His peace and joy!

"a bruised reed he will not break, and a faintly burning wick he will not quench; he will faithfully bring forth justice. He will not grow faint or be discouraged till he has established justice in the earth"
(Isaiah 42:3-4 ESV)

Jesus will not let you down, and He will not crush you or break you. He is saying He will not fail and He will not be discouraged. If you're discouraged, He will help you in your life and He will not rest till justice is in the earth!

Mary Magdalene, for example, was a prostitute and she was living in sin. Jesus forgave her and showed her love and grace and favour. She was considered very low, a scum of the earth, and unclean to people, but Jesus forgave her and delivered her and had bowels of compassion for her and countless others. He gave her hope in her life and made something beautiful of her life.

One of the Pharisees asked him to eat with him, and he went into the Pharisee's house and took his place at the table. And behold, a woman of the city, who was a sinner, when she learned that he was reclining at table in the Pharisee's house, brought an alabaster flask of ointment,and standing behind him at his feet, weeping, she began to wet his feet with her tears and wiped them with the hair of her head and kissed his feet and anointed them with the ointment. Now when the Pharisee who had invited him saw this, he said to himself, "If this man were a prophet, he would have known who and what sort of woman this is who is touching him, for she is a sinner."And Jesus answering said to him, "Simon, I have something to say to you." And he answered, "Say it, Teacher." "A certain moneylender had two debtors. One owed five hundred denarii, and the other fifty. When they could not pay, he cancelled the debt of both. Now which of them will love him more?"Simon answered, "The one, I suppose, for whom he cancelled the larger debt." And he said to him, "You have judged rightly." Then turning toward the woman he said to Simon, "Do you see this woman? I entered your house; you gave me no water for my feet, but she has wet my feet with her tears and wiped them with her hair.You gave me no kiss, but from the time I came in she has not ceased to kiss my feet. You did not anoint my head with oil, but she has anointed my feet with ointment. Therefore I tell you, her sins, which are many, are forgiven--for she loved much. But he who is forgiven little, loves little."And he said to her, "Your sins are forgiven." Then those who were at table with him began to say among themselves, "Who is this, who even forgives sins?" And he said to the woman, "Your faith has saved you; go in peace." (Luke 7:36-50 ESV).

NY Gang Leader Turned to JESUS CHRIST! - Nicky Cruz: https://www.youtube.com/watch?v=7q73yVmWbbg&t=888s

Out of the Devil's Cauldron (ex-satanist comes to Jesus): https://www.youtube.com/watch?v=tAoGlU7Uy-w

To know God's love is to let your barriers down and accept His truths, and if we draw near to Him, we trust He will draw near to us. The only way to really experience His love is to say, "Okay, God. I am here; you are the great I Am. Please show me your love." And He will! Seek Him and His Bible is not far away. That will develop your inner spirit man to grow, and you will learn to walk with Him in this life and in heaven!

People try and find happiness in every avenue of life, but it never succeeds—maybe temporary happiness, but not fulfillment. The flesh, that is our fallen nature, is never satisfied because we were designed to be in fellowship with God who is love. We all search for acceptance in one way or another; we all want more and more, either money, cars, fame, or gold.

It's things we think we want. All those things, sure, they do give some level of happiness, but once achieved, it leads to less fulfillment. So many celebrities make it and wish they never did! All their friends can become false around them over time. They have less love in their lives and more people wanting things from them. They have everything, yet they are not happy!

Billionaires and high profile business people have the drugs, the girls, the fame, so to speak, and it always turns out horrible; sometimes it leads to suicide. They reach the top and then say, "What else? What is the meaning of life? Surely there is meaning in life?" How many stories have we heard that do not end well? They eventually, at one point of their life, come to that realisation. And for some, it's sooner and some it's later that they need a change and look to a higher purpose in life, but God can use all things for good!

(Romans 8:28 ESV) says,"And we know that for those who love God all things work together for good, for those who are called according to his purpose."

There can be purposes and treasures in hard journeys that sometimes God brings about with certain circumstances in life. Some good, some bad, so as to help you on that journey to Him. Jesus is the meaning in life and Jesus is the light, but many just don't know that Jesus is the answer yet!

Let your guard down and come to the truth, and you will find that peace and acceptance you have always wanted. It is real and it is true. Don't let your past hurts stop you from going forward in this journey we call life and that which is forevermore.

There is a time coming when the real church is going to rise up and be blameless for Jesus. The world is going to see that love and be attracted to it like a magnet, a Holy Spirit magnet! That will draw people to know the true and living God. True agape love is self-sacrificing love, and the world will see its fruits.

"Beloved, let us love one another, for love is from God, and whoever loves has been born of God and knows God. Anyone who does not love does not know God, because God is love. In this the love of God was made manifest among us, that God sent his only Son into the world, so that we might live through him. In this is love, not that we have loved God but that he loved us and sent his Son to be the propitiation for our sins. Beloved, if God so loved us, we also ought to love one another."(1 John 4:7-11 ESV).

What John is saying is that God is the perfection of love. His very character is love. God cares so much about every person in this world. He says in the Bible through the psalmist David for us to understand God's heart, which is toward us.

"For You formed my inward parts;

You covered me in my mother's womb.

I will praise You, for I am fearfully and wonderfully made;

Marvellous are Your works,

And that my soul knows very well.

My frame was not hidden from You,

When I was made in secret,

And skilfully wrought in the lowest parts of the earth.

Your eyes saw my substance, being yet unformed.

And in Your book they all were written,

The days fashioned for me,

When as yet there were none of them.

"How precious also are Your thoughts to me, O God!

How great is the sum of them!

If I should count them, they would be more in number than the sand;

When I awake, I am still with You" (Psalm 139:13-18).

More than all the grains of sand! These are His thoughts towards us. God wants to know you personally and He wants to have a living relationship with you. He wants to draw you into His presence and keep you safe. He wants to teach you His ways of life and He wants to adorn you with everything He has.

"Live!' I made you flourish like a plant of the field. And you grew up and became tall and arrived at full adornment. Your breasts were formed, and your hair had grown; yet you were naked and bare." (Ezekiel 16:6-7 ESV).

He is talking about His chosen people, and it expresses His personality of love toward His people in His vine.

"When I passed by you again and saw you, behold, you were at the age for love, and I spread the corner of my garment over you and covered your

nakedness; I made my vow to you and entered into a covenant with you, declares the Lord GOD, and you became mine. Then I bathed you with water and washed off your blood from you and anointed you with oil. I clothed you also with embroidered cloth and shod you with fine leather. I wrapped you in fine linen and covered you with silk.And I adorned you with ornaments and put bracelets on your wrists and a chain on your neck. And I put a ring on your nose and earrings in your ears and a beautiful crown on your head.Thus you were adorned with gold and silver, and your clothing was of fine linen and silk and embroidered cloth. You ate fine flour and honey and oil. You grew exceedingly beautiful and advanced to royalty. And your renown went forth among the nations because of your beauty, for it was perfect through the splendor that I had bestowed on you, declares the Lord GOD. (Ezekiel 16:8-14 ESV).
You can listen to that on the Word of Promise app to get a better understanding of context.

There's just a few grains of sand expressed!

"the LORD appeared to him from far away. I have loved you with an everlasting love; therefore I have continued my faithfulness to you. Again I will build you, and you shall be built" (Jeremiah 31:3-4 ESV).

"'The LORD your God is in your midst, a mighty one who will save; he will rejoice over you with gladness; he will quiet you by his love; he will exult over you with loud singing. I will gather those of you who mourn for the festival, so that you will no longer suffer reproach. Behold, at that time I will deal with all your oppressors. And I will save the lame and gather the outcast, and I will change their shame into praise and renown in all the earth. At that time I will bring you in, at the time when I gather you together; for I will make you renowned and praised among all the peoples of the earth, when I restore your fortunes before your eyes," says the LORD." (Zephaniah 3:17-20 ESV).

"He brought me to the banqueting house,
And his banner over me was love" (Song of Songs 2:4 ESV).

" But you, O Lord, are a God merciful and gracious, slow to anger and abounding in steadfast love and faithfulness.Turn to me and be gracious to me; give your strength to your servant, and save the son of your maidservant.Show me a sign of your favor, that those who hate me may see and be put to shame because you, LORD, have helped me and comforted me." (Psalm 86:15-17 ESV).

"Your steadfast love, O LORD, extends to the heavens, your faithfulness to the clouds.Your righteousness is like the mountains of God; your judgments are like the great deep; man and beast you save, O LORD. How precious is your steadfast love, O God! The children of mankind take refuge in the shadow of your wings. They feast on the abundance of your house, and you give them drink from the river of your delights.For with you is the fountain of life; in your light do we see light."(Psalm 36:5-9 ESV).

But you are a God ready to forgive, gracious and merciful, slow to anger and abounding in steadfast love, and did not forsake them." (Nehemiah 9:17 ESV).

I will make a covenant of peace with them. It shall be an everlasting covenant with them. And I will set them in their land and multiply them, and will set my sanctuary in their midst forevermore. My dwelling place shall be with them, and I will be their God, and they shall be my people." (Ezekiel 37:26-27 ESV).

"Seek the LORD while he may be found; call upon him while he is near; let the wicked forsake his way, and the unrighteous man his thoughts; let him return to the LORD, that he may have compassion on him, and to our God, for he will abundantly pardon. For my thoughts are not your thoughts, neither are your ways my ways, declares the LORD. For as the heavens are higher than the earth, so are my ways higher than your ways and my thoughts than your thoughts.'" (Isaiah 55:6-9 ESV).

"Come to me, all who labor and are heavy laden, and I will give you rest. Take my yoke upon you, and learn from me, for I am gentle and lowly in heart, and you will find rest for your souls. For my yoke is easy, and my burden is light.'" (Matthew 11:28-30 ESV).

If you learn the history and God's lessons in the Bible, these Bible verses will mean a lot to you over time. You will come to understand that God is love and kindness and He shows favour to many! He leads from example, and He really does show His love in every aspect of life if we let Him.

Psalms 106-107 is a great overview of the love, mercy, and help He gave to the Hebrews even when they rebelled. Anyone can be a part of this new olive tree and be welcomed into His family.

The Bible is a book of love, and the only way to know Jesus and the author of life is to know Him personally! That starts with His Word to help you develop your new inner man and to grow in Him. Then He will reveal His love to you as you seek Him and He will surely draw near to you!

CHAPTER 8
How does faith work?
And what is faith?

We've made it this far; how are you enjoying this book? I hope you have let everything sink in! Let's get into what faith is.

Faith is trust, and we have faith in things every day without realising it. When you sit down, you put faith in that chair that it won't collapse. Even though you don't know who built the chair, you still trust in its quality. Have you been on an aeroplane? You put your faith in the pilots, the mechanics, the fuelers, and the engineers!

Do you know that God gives you the faith you need for salvation and your needs? And you have faith in a measure according to your need?

"For by grace you have been saved through faith, and that not of yourselves; it is the gift of God, not of works, lest anyone should boast" (Ephesians 2:8-9).

But you must use your faith as a skydiver jumps out of an aeroplane: He has a parachute and he pulls the string! He uses his parachute in accordance with his understanding of it.

The Bible promotes faith, and the rhema Word is alive, and as you get into the Bible, it is a spiritual book that is alive! It's not just the logos, which is the written Word, but the logos leads to the rhema Word with the Holy Spirit!

"So then faith comes by hearing, and hearing by the word [rhema] of God" (Romans 10:17).

The Holy Spirit is implying that faith comes from God Himself from the rhema Word of God. Rhema means "utterance" or "thing said."

Notice that the Bible says faith comes by hearing, and when Paul wrote this, there were no audiobooks in 57 AD! faith comes by hearing and that can mean an inspired preacher or a prophet or whomever God decides to speak through. It's not necessarily always Scripture, but the Holy Spirit living within you can speak to your heart or mind, or in dreams or visions. There are so many ways the Holy Spirit can speak to you: even a gentle leading or a knowing about a particular situation or "gut feel." We are to be in a living relationship with the Holy Spirit daily!

So what is the logos word and what is the rhema word? Why do we make a distinction between the logos and the rhema?

The Bible is logos. Think of it this way: the logos is the written Word of God that communicates to us and teaches us wisdom, shows us His plans, and shares stories of His love to build faith and confidence in Him from His past acts of helping mankind, like how God helped David defeat Goliath! That can help build your faith by seeing His faithfulness in the past to help you grow and trust God from His logos Word too!

"So it was, as the multitude pressed about Him to hear the word [Logos] of God …" (Luke 5:1).

Logos is a Greek word meaning "word," "reason," or "plan."

Now to apply that understanding and have a spiritual practical understanding. Imagine the logos words in the Bible that are on the pages can come to life from the Holy Spirit speaking them to you as you need empowerment in life to fulfill your calling!

As the Holy Spirit speaks to your heart and as **He wills** for what's needed in your life, **He speaks** the rhema word to you. That goes into your spirit man because we have fellowship with the Holy Spirit who is living within us if we have accepted Jesus Christ as our Saviour! The Holy Spirit can breathe on the logos words you read and will inspire your mind with His living word, rhema. That's why it's important to meditate on God's word!

"But you shall meditate in it day and night, that you may observe to do according to all that is written in it. For then you will make your way prosperous, and then you will have good success" (Joshua 1:8).

The Holy Spirit can give you the rhema word to enter your mind from the written word, logos. Then He can turn the logos word in your mind into a living spiritual word to go deep within your spirit man and to allow that rhema word to germinate in your heart and mind. Once the Holy Spirit speaks to you, that is a rhema word and it will become alive and start to grow that seed of belief because He told you! And it grows within you for it to become powerful and living and to be able to manifest into our reality!

"For as he thinks in his heart, so is he" (Proverbs 23:7).

Think about the mind—every great idea starts in the mind! Before coming into reality, let's look at engineering and the Empire State Building! William Lamb started the design of the building, and within two weeks, he had finished the design and the thought he had manifested into a blueprint from his mind to his hand! And then that led into reality! Now William Lamb had the faith within himself to get the job done, and he acted on his faith in his training and skill. I know I am speaking in material concepts, but the same can be applied to spiritual concepts within the Holy Spirit and His will!

"For everyone who partakes only of milk is unskilled in the word of righteousness, for he is a babe. But solid food belongs to those who are of full age, that is, those who by reason of use have their senses exercised to discern both good and evil"
(Hebrews 5:13-14).

The Word of God says we can be skilled in the Scriptures, just like Jesus was when He was being tempted in the desert by the devil. He used the logos that led to the rhema word and made it powerful and living in order to resist the devil and not eat or drink for forty days and forty nights, just like Moses. He lived on the Word of God. We are supernatural beings if we are in Jesus Christ because Jesus Christ is the God of the supernatural and natural, and we are to be His disciples and imitate Him. That is faith in Jesus and trusting Him that what He promises He keeps and not go by sight but by faith and to live forever with Him in eternity!

"It is written, 'Man shall not live by bread alone, but by every word that proceeds from the mouth of God' " (Matthew 4:4).

"If you can believe, all things are possible to him who believes" (Mark 9:23).

"For the word of God is living and powerful, and sharper than any two-edged sword, piercing even to the division of soul and spirit, and of joints and marrow!" (Hebrews 4:12).

God's Word is powerful and ready to do His will! Put simply, faith is given to you for salvation and your needs in life! So don't worry if you say you don't have enough faith for anything because God is the God who gives faith by hearing His Word.

For example, if I tell you I am going to give you $100 next week, and you trust my word that what I say I will do, your next week's budget is going to factor in that $100 in faith because I am creditable or worthy to be believed. So you may be able to plan to buy extra groceries or treat yourself out to a meal or a movie for a date night! I gave you the faith to be able to put into action your plans for where you're going and what you're going to do with that $100.

Businesses operate all the time with trusting suppliers and manufacturers and loans from banks!

Well, God is the same way. You don't need to "make up" your own faith and grow your faith in your own efforts! God will give you the faith you need in His context, not your own, and allow you to believe according to Him saying so and giving you faith to ask Him!

Do you know God says in His Word the Holy Bible: "I will be with you. I will not leave you nor forsake you. Be strong and of good courage" (Joshua 1:5-6)? Meditate on that and trust God to make that Scripture alive to you and expect Him to bring it to pass!

God visited Abraham and told him in person that Sarah would bear a child. She laughed! Because she was barren, Abraham did not just randomly make up that idea, although he was very much wanting the Lord to give him a child! God gave him the faith to believe! Sure, Abraham did go on travels without knowing completely where he was going, but God first told him to leave! Sometimes we know exactly what God promises and sometimes it's a journey that God uses to test and stretch our faith to see if the faith He gives us will be more precious than gold. Abraham waited twenty-five years!

"In this you greatly rejoice, though now for a little while, if need be, you have been grieved by various trials, that the genuineness of your faith, being much more precious than gold that perishes, though it is tested by fire, may be found to praise, honor, and glory at the revelation of Jesus Christ, whom having not seen you love. Though now you do not see Him, yet believing, you rejoice with joy inexpressible and full of glory, receiving the end of your faith—the salvation of your souls" 1 Peter 1:6-9).

To grow in steadfastness and stamina in Jesus is to trust in Him and persist in believing what He says He will do. The devil will try to get you to doubt just like with Ishmael and Abraham. That's fine; doubt will try and come, but that does not disqualify you if you doubt.

It's a matter of knowing what God has said and standing on the rhema word of God and learning to enter into His rest. One preacher I know said sometimes it's like being in a boxing ring. Just because it doesn't happen straight away doesn't mean it's not God's will: you need to have that stamina in the boxing ring to press on and believe God to deliver whatever may be promised to you! Not always does God require refining for His plans. His purpose may be quick just like that guy in the video I played before; he simply asked God in faith and Jesus healed him overnight and the doctors told him to go home!

"'For My thoughts are not your thoughts,

Nor are your ways My ways,' says the LORD.

'For as the heavens are higher than the earth,

So are My ways higher than your ways,

And My thoughts than your thoughts'" (Isaiah 55:8-9).

The Bible is full of promises; all you need to do is ask God and trust Him, and God will open your spiritual eyes to be able to believe His words just like Moses. He had a tunnel view; he did not look in the middle, but he looked at the end. Having that mindset enabled him to look beyond his natural understanding!

"By faith he forsook Egypt, not fearing the wrath of the king; for he endured as seeing Him who is invisible" (Hebrews 11:27).

Faith does not need to be complicated; it is very simple, God cannot lie! So be like a little child to say, "Okay, God, show me what I need to know and help me become full of faith like a little child with their parents looking after them and in faith and great expectation of my prayers to be answered." That is having a living relationship with Him and getting to know Him personally!

Faith comes by hearing the Word of God and knowing His ways. He has laid out a foundation in the Bible to get to know Him. Then your relationship and faith with Him can grow quickly! First you will be as a baby, then you will mature and learn to walk in love and your faith in Him will grow. The more you lay a firmer foundation of His truths and renew your mind to Jesus, the more your faith will be more confident and steady in Jesus!

Faith is gentle, faith is firm, faith is guidance, and faith is best kept simple!

Jesus's teachings were very simple but also complex to those who have hardened hearts! The Bible and the Holy Spirit are the best teachers, and God will open and soften people's hearts slowly! The more you get into the Bible, the more seeds you will allow the Holy Spirit to plant and grow within you, and the more your faith will grow!

CHAPTER 9
The Trinity explained

Okay! So Joel, what is the Trinity?

God is omniscient, omnipotent, and omnipresent. Using our limited understanding, how can there be three persons but yet One God?

I've heard about Jesus and the Father, now the Holy Spirit! Are there three Gods? Simply put, no.

You may know that this book has been for anybody who wants to get a closer understanding about salvation and the history of the world with the Bible's perspective. How it all connects with life and with our traditions and culture, and some tough questions about sin and how important it is to know the author of life: Jesus, the author and finisher of our faith! But now we must understand the Godhead is three persons but one being that makes up God. In short, with geek talk: the Trinity.

The Trinity of God is like this!

We are made in the image of God. So let's relate it to us in our dimensions! We have a **body, soul, and spirit**. Imagine the Father as the body, then next imagine Jesus as the soul, and thirdly imagine the Holy Spirit, like our spirit, our life that God breathed into us, so that makes three in one. Since we are made in the image of God, it makes sense to explain the Trinity that way!

Some mathematicians have worked out that we live in an up to eleven-dimensional universe. God is so interesting as He created maths, quantum physics, computer algorithms, and DNA!

All the things in this world we love, He ultimately created! He gives knowledge and understanding. Look in the last 150 years with the leaps and bounds we have made Like He said, He will speed up the time and knowledge will increase and we will go all around the world, as if He knew!

"Many shall run to and fro, and knowledge shall increase" (Daniel 12:4).

Okay, the Godhead! Since God created these dimensions, we have found out how God is three in one. He is omnipotent (unlimited power), omnipresent (He is everywhere), and Omniscient (all knowing). That is who God is. He is outside of our universe that we know of, and since we live in a dimensional universe, He must be ridiculously smart to be able to create what we know as life. So I tend to think nothing is impossible for Him because He is the programmer! For those tech guys, it's actually said we live in a digital organic/spiritual hologram and outside of this universe is where the real reality is! That can sound crazy, but the more science finds, the more it goes with the Bible!

Oh wait, sorry, I got excited; it's my inner nerd! Back to the Trinity of God and dimensions! It does relate!

It's been found we can have up to an eleven-dimensional universe, which we humans cannot understand. At the best, we understand only four dimensions. The fifth dimension we cannot wrap our head around without a complex explanation, and then we can sort of explain it.

So if you understand where I'm going here with the dimensions, then imagine God is unlimited dimensions. That is how He can be everywhere. He can be in human form and still be the Father or the Holy Spirit. That's how there can be three but all are one God! Although they, the father, Jesus, the Holy Spirit all have individual personalities and wills. We are limited in our three dimensions that we can understand! We cannot grasp it. It's like trying to describe to a 2-D stickman drawing what it's like to live in 3-D reality! Imagine you are saying to the stickman, "Well, underneath that a4 paper of white is the floor where I am from" He would be like, "What!!! Are you talking about, dude? It's white paper and nothing else can be underneath me but white paper." You would make that stickman very confused! We can comprehend it because we live in these dimensions. But we cannot comprehend God's dimensions and how He operates and sees us in this world and universe, but I'm glad I can't understand. That makes Him God and not me But one day I'll ask!

Creation Argument for the existence of God:
https://www.youtube.com/watch?v=8_OC2t7mIWE

Chuck Missler can go more into that in this video!
Ten Dimensional Universe - Chuck Missler:
https://www.youtube.com/watch?v=bHwkKckFgx0

Quantum Physics We Live in a Hologram: there are many videos on YouTube with this topic. Check it out on YouTube! Juan Maldacena blows our reality!

Brian Greene and Leonard Susskind - Holographic Principle:
https://www.youtube.com/watch?v=A_GpwjQU2Jo

"At a black hole, **Albert Einstein's** theory of gravity apparently clashes with quantum physics, but that conflict could be solved if the **Universe** were a **holographic** projection. A team of physicists has provided some of the clearest evidence yet that our **Universe** could be just one big projection."

(Reference for quote)
https://www.nature.com/news/simulations-back-up-theory-that-universe-is-a-hologram-1.14328

CHAPTER 10
How can I be saved?

It's very simple! Even though some of those details are a bit to go into, I hope it gives you a firmer foundation if you choose to give your life to Jesus. It can help you understand why He is so important in this life. We only have one life here, and it's so important to seek the truth out to continue with Him. Rather than being separated from Him in judgment, we have an opportunity to know Him forever.

"For with the heart one believes unto righteousness, and with the mouth confession is made unto salvation." For the Scripture says, 'Whoever believes in Him will not be put to shame.' For there is no distinction between Jew and Greek, for the same Lord over all is rich to all who call upon Him. For 'whoever calls on the name of the Lord shall be saved'" (Romans 10:10-13).

Jesus can save anyone, the worst of the worst—it doesn't matter. His blood covers all sins! If you really mean you're sorry and you want to turn from your past ways, He will most definitely forgive and forget your sins and He will remember them no more! If you want to become a Son or daughter of God and Let God take you legally away from the wicked one the devil, to be hidden with Jesus in His Love and tender mercy's he will, but you must be willing, for he will delight to crown you with his riches of love and righteousness if you accept His free gift that he has provided for you.

"Who is a God like You,
Pardoning iniquity
And passing over the transgression of the remnant of His heritage?
He does not retain His anger forever,
Because He delights in mercy.
He will again have compassion on us,
And will subdue our iniquities.
You will cast all our sins
Into the depths of the sea.
You will give truth to Jacob

And mercy to Abraham,
Which You have sworn to our fathers
From days of old" (Micah 7:18-20).

"Seek the Lord while He may be found,
Call upon Him while He is near.
Let the wicked forsake his way,
And the unrighteous man his thoughts;
Let him return to the Lord,
And He will have mercy on him;
And to our God,
For He will abundantly pardon" (Isaiah 55:6-7, emphasis added)

You simply ask Jesus for forgiveness as you would if you were talking to Him face to face. If you would like to accept Jesus, please repeat after me:

Jesus, I have sinned, and I acknowledge my sin. I am sorry, and I ask for forgiveness, and I want you to make me as white as snow as you promised you would forgive me. I want to turn from my past ways of living in sin and would like it if you would come into my heart and make me a new creation, to be born of the Spirit and have your life in me. I thank you for what you did for me on the cross, and I believe you rose from the dead and are Lord of all the earth and heaven. Amen.

Congratulations and welcome to the family of Jesus Christ!

"Then I will say to those who were not My people,
'You are My people!'
And they shall say, 'You are my God!'" (Hosea 2:23).

Remember to listen to Revelation. It's pretty interesting! Also try the app Word of Promise. John is free. At this time of publishing, you can try Audible for a thirty-day free trial. You can get The Word of Promise Bible audio there too. It really brings the Bible to life. I would like to point out that I am not sponsored by Amazon, nor Word of Promise. I just genuinely highly recommend it! One hour a night or morning for two months. It will change your life.

If you did not choose to accept Jesus, then I highly recommend you do your own research and try and keep an unbiased approach to it. Ask your heart the tough questions and be honest with yourself. I recommend the book *Case for Christ*. The author was an atheist journalist who decided to use his skills on the Bible and history to prove it false, and you will be surprised at his logical yet unbiased opinions and how he came to his conclusions. It's even been made into a movie, *Case for Christ*. I'm sure you can find a stream! It's a decent movie too! Trailer link here: https://www.youtube.com/watch?v=rhe8KhSxWGo

Thanks for reading my book, and I hope it helps you in your journey. If you enjoyed it, please give it a rating and review as it will help this book lead people to the author of life!

—Joel

Links

Links for the YouTube videos I used throughout the book.

science confirms the bible
https://www.youtube.com/watch?v=CFYswvGoaPU&t=833s

Is Genesis history?
https://www.youtube.com/watch?v=UM82qxxskZE

pneumatology john G lake
https://www.youtube.com/watch?v=9-DjvIYNe70&list=PLCyk3zOeKL
G5Q9xaaMwjiWyCiHvHnCr9R

God's Generals Series - Smith Wigglesworth
https://www.youtube.com/watch?v=51_QnZtZhmc

Elvis How great thou art 1972
https://www.youtube.com/watch?v=XlfcvUtUoOM

Pete Seeger's Rainbow Quest Hedy West, Mississippi John Hurt, Paul
Cadwell Full Episode
https://www.youtube.com/watch?v=Cd6lBQJAsEM&t=2371s

The Welsh Revival of 1904: - youtube
https://www.youtube.com/watch?v=oJOu8eUhcys

God's Generals Series - Evan Roberts: - youtube
https://www.youtube.com/watch?v=8Jp85m6yl3s

The Azusa Street Revival (Documentary): - youtube
https://www.youtube.com/watch?v=HPtGJ35jIwA

God's Generals Series - John Alexander Dowie:
https://www.youtube.com/watch?v=3hXZ_1ZtHXQ

The Devastating Effects When Prayer Was Removed From School in
America in 1962-63 - David Barton
https://www.youtube.com/watch?v=1No--GpdqCY.

Why Young People Are More Depressed Than Ever Before
https://www.youtube.com/watch?v=CPh8QoSdBPM

Testifying about Jesus to the UN General Assembly - Lee Stoneking Miracle
https://www.youtube.com/watch?v=B1mDiGy2-0g&t=168s

Miracles of God caught on tape!!!
https://www.youtube.com/watch?v=_fkvKu2In98

Drug Addict Comes Face to Face with Jesus
https://www.youtube.com/watch?v=rbpET1SRrcs

Catholicism: Worth Arguing About (1st of 4 videos on Catholicism)
https://www.youtube.com/watch?v=91n6erthX6A&list=PLZ3iRMLYFl
HvsToYQdfDkiDE6dPkouIv3

Why Catholicism is WRONG
https://www.youtube.com/watch?v=TPG3vMeexks&t=45s

Roman Catholicism: Contending for the Faith
https://www.youtube.com/watch?v=7ZVHHmCOjOg

The Crucifixion | A Medical Perspective
https://www.youtube.com/watch?v=T-EVfxABSoU

NY Gang Leader Turned to JESUS CHRIST! - Nicky Cruz
https://www.youtube.com/watch?v=7q73yVmWbbg&t=888s

Out of the Devil's Cauldron Ex satanist comes to Jesus
john ramirez testimony -
https://www.youtube.com/watch?v=tAoGlU7Uy-w

Creation Argument for the existence of God
https://www.youtube.com/watch?v=8_OC2t7mIWE

Ten Dimensional Universe - Chuck Missler:
https://www.youtube.com/watch?v=bHwkKckFgx0

Brian Greene and Leonard Susskind - Holographic Principle
https://www.youtube.com/watch?v=A_GpwjQU2Jo

The Case for Christ Official Trailer 1 (2017) - Mike Vogel Movie
https://www.youtube.com/watch?v=rhe8KhSxWGo

www.ingramcontent.com/pod-product-compliance
Lightning Source LLC
Chambersburg PA
CBHW070645030426
42337CB00020B/4166